Our Life with Birds

Our Life with Birds

A NATURE TRAILS BOOK

John Tveten & Gloria Tveten

Illustrations by John Tveten

Texas A&M University Press   COLLEGE STATION

Library of Congress Cataloging-in-Publication Data

Tveten, John L.
    Our life with birds : a nature trails book / John Tveten and
Gloria Tveten ; illustrations by John Tveten.—1st ed.
        p. cm.
    A collection of articles which originally appeared in the
Houston chronicle from 1977–1998.
        ISBN 1-58544-380-8 (cloth : alk. paper)
        1. Bird watching.   2. Birds.   I. Tveten, Gloria A., 1938–
II. Title.   III. Series.
QL677.5.T89   2004
598—dc22   2004004333

Earlier versions of these essays appeared in the *Houston Chronicle.*

To our son Michael,
who walked some of these nature trails with us
and shared many of the experiences.
Without him, the birds would not have seemed
as colorful nor sung so cheerfully.

Contents

Acknowledgments

We are indebted to many people who played a part in these adventures through the years, who took us to new places and showed us new birds. A few are mentioned in the individual accounts of our experiences, but there were far too many to adequately acknowledge. To all who traveled the nature trails with us—THANK YOU.

We want to thank our editors at the *Houston Chronicle*, of whom there were many in the twenty-four years we wrote for that newspaper. In particular, Jack Loftis first allowed us space to write about our love of nature and helped steer us in the right direction, and Jane Marshall, our last *Chronicle* editor, provided us with kind encouragement and expert guidance.

Thanks go, too, to William H. and Elsa E. Thompson, founding publishers of *Bird Watcher's Digest,* and Mark T. Adams, author of *Chasing Birds accross Texas: A Birding Big Year,* who reviewed the manuscript and offered several helpful suggestions.

We owe a special debt of gratitude to Texas A&M University Press and its staff, including editor Shannon Davies, who urged us to compile our previously published columns in book form and worked patiently with us to achieve that goal. Likewise, we thank Cynthia Lindlof, our copyeditor, who understood what we were trying to say and enabled us to say it better.

Introduction

This book is based on newspaper columns that appeared weekly in the *Houston Chronicle* under the title "Nature Trails" for more than twenty-four years, from February 15, 1975, through March 26, 1999. For this first volume, we have selected some of the columns that deal specifically with birds. We hope that in the future there will be more volumes about other forms of flora and fauna and about some of the world's most beautiful and fascinating locations to which our travels have taken us.

For the first few years, "Nature Trails" appeared under the sole credit John L. Tveten. Having just left a job as an industrial research organic chemist to start a new career as a freelance nature writer and photographer, John had the audacity to approach Jack Loftis, then feature editor of the *Chronicle,* with the idea for a weekly column. Later, Gloria took early retirement from teaching college mathematics and shared the byline. Virtually all of these adventures were shared experiences, however, and we have rewritten the early columns to reflect that fact.

Freed from the strict space constraints of a daily newspaper, we have also expanded some of the material where we felt it was warranted. In some cases, we included more than one column in series; in others, we have combined portions of two or more columns published over a period of years, rewriting them as one. Although no column was ever reprinted verbatim in the newspaper, we sometimes wrote again about a particular subject we had treated a decade or more previously, usually with new insight from personal experiences or with new data from more recent literature. Dates included with each entry indicate the year, or years, in which the original material was published.

Finally, we have added for this book parenthetical comments in italics that reflect changes in taxonomy or status or that help explain the context or content of each chapter or column. Hopefully, these will clarify nomenclature that at first may seem confusing or outdated.

There were more than 1,250 weekly columns during the tenure of "Nature Trails" in the *Chronicle*. Although the length and format of the columns varied from time to time, we estimate that we wrote more than one and one-quarter million words for our allotted space. Not all of those words, perhaps, were good literary choices, but we hope that the ones we have chosen for this book will prove informative and entertaining.

Bird Names

Awkward problems arise when using bird names in different styles of writing. The "official names," as dictated by the American Ornithologists' Union (AOU) in their checklist, are capitalized when used in their entirety: Common Loon, Eastern Screech-Owl, Black-necked Stilt, or Scissor-tailed Flycatcher. However, the more general forms, without the specific names—loon, screech-owl, stilt, or flycatcher—appear without that capitalization. Scientific works, including most field guides and journals dealing specifically with birds, follow this convention. Ornithologists argue that it reduces confusion, making it clear that the word "common" in "Common Loon" is part of the name and not a simple adjective reflecting the bird's abundance or distribution.

Most popular writing follows a more literary style in which the names are not capitalized. This includes newspaper and magazine articles, as well as many books intended for the general public. The columns included here were originally published in the latter style, without capitalization of the names.

Both systems have their merits. The scientific form serves to prevent confusion, but it is visually awkward. The full names of the American Robin and Northern Mockingbird, for example, are capitalized; however, they revert to lowercase when they become simply robin or mockingbird, which is often the case. It would be unusual to use the complete names more than once or twice in a popular article before falling back to the more generic references. Even more jarring is a list of bird names that uses both, as for a group of shorebirds on the beach: Long-billed Curlews, Sanderlings, knots (only one species in the United States, and seldom specified as Red Knot), Piping Plovers, and dowitchers (of undetermined species).

Equally confusing is the acceptable form for abbreviations of the proper name. In referring to the Ivory-billed Woodpecker, for example, some authors capitalize the abbreviated form, Ivory-bill. Others do not, because that is not the official AOU name.

The capitalized bird names seem particularly awkward when writing about a wide variety of flora and fauna. In most cases, only the bird names are so treated, although the butterfly names recently approved by the North American Butterfly Association share that style. There are no such universally accepted standards for most other taxa. Thus, the reader is certain to wonder why the name of a Red-shouldered Hawk is capitalized, but that of the post oak in which it perches is not, nor are the green treefrog and southern flying squirrel that share the hawk's leafy refuge.

For these reasons, we have chosen not to use the capitalized forms of bird names and to reproduce them as they appeared in the original newspaper columns. We realize this choice may offend some ornithologists and ardent birders, but we also believe it makes the writing style less awkward and pretentious.

Our Life with Birds

1

The Joy of Birding

Although dedicated birders always seek to add new birds to their lists and the discovery of a species never before seen may provide the highlight of any day afield, the true joy of birding lies, at least for us, in the simple enjoyment of the world's avian riches. As we have often said: We enjoy seeing uncommon birds, but we also enjoy seeing common birds doing uncommon things. And, most of all, we simply enjoy birds being birds uncommonly well.

The following columns reflect the joy that comes from watching birds, whether they are common or rare. Such moments await wherever you may be, and their pursuit promises a lifetime of treasured memories.

Minnesota Summer: 1988

We are sprawled in chairs on the porch, looking out through white-trunked birches and gnarled oaks to the lake beyond. Binoculars and cool drinks rest beside us on the deck; our feet are propped comfortably on the rail. It is a tough business, this bird-watching, here among the blue lakes and rugged woodlands of northern Minnesota.

We should, we suppose, be out pursuing species new to our lists. The spruce grouse has been known to nest in the region, and the rare black-backed woodpecker occasionally frequents stands of pines in the forests nearby. Both are species we have not as yet seen.

But it is comfortable here, and the more common birds are always a delight. We are content to share our leisure time with them.

We understand the enthusiasm of the ardent "birders," as the listers now prefer to call themselves, and we, too, enjoy seeing new and unusual species. But we are still "bird-watchers" at heart, for we find our old avian friends as fascinating as the new.

Perched on the rail nearby is an eastern phoebe, one of a pair that nested earlier in the season atop a light fixture beneath the second-story deck. It is nervous about our presence, yet curious, too, and we eye each other with mutual interest. At the same time, a dapper white-breasted nuthatch forages up and down the trunk of a birch a few feet away. It appears never to have heard of gravity, and it seems as comfortable feeding head downward as in the more traditional way.

A tiny hummingbird hovers in front of us, ruby throat glistening in the sun. He repeatedly approaches a wire hanging near the rail, where in previous seasons a feeder hung. The hummingbird

White-breasted nuthatch

apparently remembers that feeder, for there is nothing to attract him now; Gloria's parents have chosen to hang the feeders elsewhere around their home.

From its customary perch on a dead limb near the edge of the woods, a broad-winged hawk launches into a swooping dive and lands abruptly at the base of the lakeside dock. Through our binoculars we can see it struggling to subdue a rodent, probably a bog lemming; however, it flies off again with its prey clutched in its sharp talons before we can get a better look.

A male eastern bluebird perches on a post in the raspberry patch below us, slowly and carefully selecting the largest and ripest berries for his meal. It is comical to watch him pick a berry and swallow it whole, gulping and gasping with the too-large berry wedged in his mouth, all the while seemingly trying to maintain a dapper demeanor.

Sated, he drops to a patch of sunlit grass and sprawls full length, tail and wings spread wide to the warming rays. For several minutes he lies there motionless, and we watch enthralled, for we have not seen a bluebird sunbathe in quite this fashion. Each iridescent feather glows blue as if lit by an internal flame. Finally, the bluebird rouses himself as if from a trance, looks around for a moment, and then flies off to a shady perch on a birch limb. There he begins to preen, carefully cleaning and arranging each feather after his day at the beach.

Meanwhile, the female bluebird appears with an enormous grasshopper clamped in her beak, the insect's black-and-white wings still beating furiously, and its powerful legs kicking. Landing atop the shed, the bird proceeds to pound the grasshopper into submission against the roof. Stopping to examine her prey intently, she detects some slight movement, and another round of pounding begins.

The female is then joined by a young bluebird just out of the nest. Hints of blue in the wings and tail reveal its identity, but the back and breast are still heavily spotted. Crying piteously and fluttering its wings, the juvenile begs to be fed. Its mother, however, picks up the grasshopper and flies off into a thicket, pursued by the still-screaming youngster.

Our quiet, restful afternoon is filled with brilliant American goldfinches and purple finches in breeding plumage, industrious yellow-bellied sapsuckers and hairy woodpeckers, cedar waxwings, scores of vireos of several species, and a dozen kinds of warblers. In our all-too-short stay we catalog fifty-four different species of birds without really working at building that list. With their colorful plumage and ceaseless antics, they add enormously to our vacation enjoyment.

A Day on the Texas Gulf Coast: 1998

The great blue heron stalks slowly along the beachfront in the shallow water, its long neck drawn back in a graceful curve and its slate gray plumage ruffled by a brisk onshore breeze. Nearby, a snowy egret stirs the sandy bottom with its golden feet, hoping to startle small fish into ill-advised flight.

A white ibis prowls the water's edge, poking and probing amid the spartina grass for the fiddler crabs that scuttle back and forth in panic. Reaching deep into a crab burrow with its long, decurved pink bill, the ibis deftly extracts the wriggling occupant and, after beating it several times against the ground, wolfs down the tasty morsel, claws and all.

From our third-floor balcony at the Laguna Reef Hotel in Rockport, Texas, we are witnesses to an avian parade of amazing diversity. Enormous brown pelicans wheel to dive headlong into the surf in pursuit of fish, and colorful roseate spoonbills sail past almost within reach as they settle into the surrounding marsh.

There are tricolored and little blue herons, great egrets, willets, dowitchers, and ruddy turnstones near the fishing pier that stretches far out into Aransas Bay. A dapper Wilson's plover strolls across the grass in front of the hotel, and a family of oystercatchers parades along an exposed shell spit nearby.

Rockport has long been known as a fisherman's paradise and as a family vacation spot, but summer vacation is now over, and most of the children have returned to school. The town is relatively quiet as it basks under a warm Texas sun. One of Rockport's major resources, however, draws people from across the continent at every season of the year. This is one of the richest birding locations in the nation, and the community has made a concerted effort to cater to both its avian residents and the tourists who come to see them.

Most famous, certainly, are the whooping cranes that spend the winter at the Aransas National Wildlife Refuge and in the adjacent

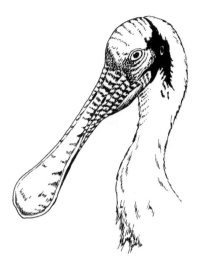

Roseate spoonbill

coastal marshes. Several boats based in the Rockport-Fulton area provide close-up views of these magnificent endangered birds along with the myriad waterfowl and shorebirds that also move down from the North in autumn. During the summer, those same boats offer tours to rookery islands with their concentrations of nesting herons, egrets, spoonbills, and ibises, as well as an assortment of gulls, terns, and skimmers.

Spring migration brings flocks of colorful warblers, tanagers, buntings, and orioles across the coastline to rest and feed in the wind-swept live oaks that ornament the picturesque seaside landscape, and that flow reverses during fall migration. As we sit watching from our balcony, the air is filled with swallows moving southward along the coast. Barn, cliff, and tree swallows drift past by the hundreds, pausing briefly to hawk insects in midair, then resume their unerring flight toward their winter refuges in the Neotropics.

Ruby-throated hummingbirds, too, move through in enormous numbers each September, building up along the bay front and then striking out on favorable winds to venture deep into Mexico and Central America. The human residents of Rockport-Fulton fully realize the value of these tiniest of birds and plant nectar-rich flowers and put out feeders that attract buzzing hordes to their backyards.

Capitalizing on this resource, the local chamber of commerce sponsors a four-day Hummer/Bird Celebration that takes place each September. Bus and boat tours, lectures on birds and other facets of natural history, and scores of booths with nature-related items vie for everyone's attention.

The stars of the Celebration, however, are the hummingbirds themselves, and they never fail to delight the crowds. Last year's event, the ninth such festival, attracted five thousand people, who contributed an estimated $1.6 million to the local economy. Our native birds are not only invaluable to our environment but can be a very good business investment.

The avian riches of Rockport were first brought to the attention of the ornithological community by a woman named Martha Conger ("Connie") Neblett Hagar, who moved there in 1934 with her husband, Jack Hagar, and bought a small cabin court, the Rockport Cottages. Connie soon began twice-daily rounds of bird-watching, and the unusual species and sheer numbers of the birds she reported amazed everyone.

Many experts of that time doubted Hagar's claims, until they came to Rockport to see for themselves. And they still come to this day, on organized birding tours and on their own vacation schedules, from far and wide, to revel in whooping cranes and hummingbirds, in spoonbills and skimmers.

By legislative act in December 1943, the Connie Hagar Wildlife Sanctuary was established in what is known locally as Little Bay. Gulls, terns, and other waterbirds nest on the islands in this refuge managed by the Texas Parks and Wildlife Department, while the bay waters attract enormous flocks of wintering redheads and canvasbacks and such local specialties as black-bellied whistling-ducks.

More recently, the nonprofit Friends of Connie Hagar purchased the original site of the Rockport Cottages. Managed as a migratory bird sanctuary, this six-and-one-half-acre wooded tract has an observation tower overlooking the coastal oaks, and its short birding trails are open to the public. The same group also created and maintains, with the cooperation of the Texas Department of Transportation, a hummingbird demonstration garden, a berry-producing garden for other birds, and a wetlands pond with a short boardwalk.

All of these sites have been designated as stops on the Great Texas Coastal Birding Trail, and the Hummer/Bird Celebration has served as a model for numerous other birding festivals throughout Texas and across the nation.

The Rockport area is blessed with an active chamber of commerce that understands nature tourism and works closely with dedicated and seemingly tireless nature groups and a community that has become increasingly aware of the riches that surround it.

Clearly, such efforts to preserve natural habitats and increase environmental awareness offer huge rewards, both for the human inhabitants of this small coastal town and for the birds with which they share it. We, too, enjoy these rewards as we sit quietly on our balcony overlooking Aransas Bay and watch the myriad bird species that pass in review. We see no "lifers," birds new to our lists, on this balmy, sunlit day, but we revel in watching countless old friends and their endlessly fascinating antics.

A National Champion Bird Tree: 1990

We have always had a fascination for trees, and over the past few years we have searched for and photographed many of the state and national champions, the largest of their species. Recently, we found another tree that proved to be a champion, but not because of its size. This one is a world-class bird tree.

It is not very imposing to look at. Most of it is dead, with only a few small green shoots arising from the base. A willow, it has three main trunks, none more than four inches in diameter. Those trunks reach a height of only fifteen feet, and the leafless branches are thickly covered with lichens of green and orange and pale blue.

Our champion willow stands beside a one-lane dirt road in northern Minnesota's Hubbard County, a rutted trail that no one but a bird-watcher would venture down. A little seep at the tree's base waters wild purple iris, spotted touch-me-not, and a thick stand of lush green sedges.

We would not have stopped had we not heard a common yellowthroat singing from among those sedges. From the open car window we made a series of the squeaks and kissing sounds that birders use to attract their quarry. The yellowthroat immediately hopped up onto a limb of the tree to get a closer look at the invaders of his territory and posed nicely for a portrait.

As we were about to drive on, another little bird appeared, a male mourning warbler. Our squeaks next brought out a curious catbird from the nearby brush, and there was even more furtive activity beyond. We quickly changed our plans for the remainder of the afternoon and pulled the car off into the shallow ditch about twenty feet from the tree. Telephoto lens braced atop a sandbag on the window, we settled down comfortably to wait. The results amazed us.

A number of flycatchers of various sizes stopped by to perch in the top branches and watch for flying insects. An eastern kingbird was the largest and most aggressive, ruling the roost when it was there and allowing no other intruders. There were also eastern phoebes and wood-pewees, the latter with pronounced wing bars, the former without. The smallest, a least flycatcher, returned from time to time to feed not only on insects but on the white fruits of a little dogwood at the base of the tree. This latter flycatcher was a real treat, for all too often we must dismiss the species and its close relatives as simply "*Empidonax* sp." Now, however, it sat and sang for us, a dry and less-than-melodious *chebek,* but definitive nonetheless.

A song sparrow, true to its name, perched frequently on a limb and sang its pleasant refrain. It alternated between the tree and a fence post across the road, apparently watching over a nest tucked securely into the grass.

A swamp sparrow visited only once, but chipping sparrows repeatedly landed in the tree and then dropped down to a bush nearby. They were carrying insects to their young, and when we listened carefully, we could hear the plaintive, hungry cries each time a parent approached. Loath to disturb them, we made no sudden moves in their direction.

Within an hour, we met a dapper pair of American redstarts, an indigo bunting in dress blues, a small flock of American goldfinches, a red-eyed vireo, and a downy woodpecker that came to search for insects beneath the flaking bark. A pair of yellow warblers, fledglings in tow, made a brief visit, and a black-billed cuckoo came to watch us intently for several minutes before dropping to

Common yellowthroat

the ground beside the front tire of our car to snatch a caterpillar.

In a quiet moment, we tried to figure out why this one small tree was so popular. On the edge of a clear-cut woodland now grown up in brush, and near a dense forest of aspens and conifers, it apparently provided a convenient lookout post as birds moved from the shelter of the forest to the wet meadow and hay field across the road. It was an isolated perch at the crossroads, a place from which to survey their world and watch for both enemies and food.

Before dusk, we had made friends with a group of cedar waxwings and four young bluebirds that also dust-bathed in the road. A male ruby-throated hummingbird perched repeatedly on the very tip of the highest branch. There were northern orioles, barn swallows, red-winged blackbirds, and a pretty chestnut-sided warbler.

It is not much of a tree, this willow of ours, but it will always be a world champion in our minds. In its branches it harbored an astonishing array of avian visitors, and it provided us with a truly enjoyable afternoon.

We returned to this dead willow the following year in June, again with rewarding results. The next year, however, the little tree was gone, presumably rotted away at its water-soaked base and lost among the thick sedges and irises from which it grew. Yellowthroats still sang from the marshy edge, and waxwings and bluebirds still perched nearby. But there seemed to be no central assembly point for these various species; the bird tree now exists only in our photos and in our memories.

Birders of All Ages: 1985

Spring migration is unquestionably the highlight of the ornithological year along our Texas coast. Birders from across the state and, indeed, from across the continent meet here in April and early May to enjoy the colorful warblers, tanagers, buntings, and orioles that stream across the Gulf of Mexico from their winter homes in the Central and South American tropics. These crowds of assembled bird-watchers are indicative of the enormous popularity of our wonderful sport.

It is eight o'clock on a cool, cloudy Saturday morning when we arrive at the Louis Smith Bird Sanctuary in High Island. Owned and operated by the Houston Audubon Society, the sanctuary was purchased in 1981 and provides some of the area's best birding. A woodland motte atop a salt dome rising out of the coastal marsh at the base of the Bolivar Peninsula, it offers a haven for tired and hungry migrants that have flown nonstop across the Gulf.

This is not a particularly good birding day, for the strong southeasterly winds have aided the migratory journey, and many of the birds have continued inland without stopping. However, there is a sizable crowd of people on hand, and we park far up the road at the end of a long line of cars. Birders may well outnumber their quarry on this late April morning.

We first encounter a young couple from Houston, who have just seen their first indigo bunting. They are ecstatic with this electric-blue bird, and we share that enthusiasm no matter how many times we have seen the species. It is one of nature's supreme attractions, without a doubt.

A young man from Beaumont is quick to share his sightings with us. He has been here just a little while and has listed only six species. "But three of them are ones I have never seen before," he says. We wander on and leave him gazing in amazement at an almost fluorescent scarlet tanager.

Two young boys race up to their parents standing nearby. "We just saw an oriole," they exclaim with a shout, "or maybe it was a grosbeak. Oh wow, it was pretty!" And they dart off again down the path, a shared binocular passing from hand to hand. On such youthful enthusiasm rests the future of our wildlife and its vital habitat. Birding is one sport in which increasing participation is in the best interests of both the hunter and the hunted. It is encouraging to see new people studying nature in the field.

We leave the sanctuary for a time to pursue, without success, a flock of scoters and a rare Arctic tern reported by others from the beach and then return to the woods in the afternoon. By now it is threatening to rain, but the crowd is larger than before.

We talk briefly with old friends from Corpus Christi, who are here with a group led by Gene Blacklock of Welder Wildlife Refuge, and with a Victor Emanuel Nature Tour led by noted Texas birder John Arvin. There are field-trip groups from Dallas and Austin, and ornithology professor Keith Arnold is here with his students from Texas A&M University. Many of these are longtime acquaintances, and it is like a class reunion or a family picnic. We tell someone we are "birding for birders rather than for birds." It is one of the joys of spring migration, this meeting of old friends.

During a brief shower, some of us stand crowded together beneath the roof of the information kiosk, comparing notes and watching a group of orioles foraging through the rain in a nearby mulberry tree. A bearded man who joins us looks familiar, and we realize it is Benton Basham, who in 1983 set the North American record by seeing a seemingly impossible 711 bird species in a single year.

In that quest, he journeyed twice to fabled Attu Island off Alaska to see such Eurasian vagrants as the rustic bunting, dusky thrush, and Siberian rubythroat. He sought out a stray tropical parula and a clay-colored robin in Texas' Rio Grande Valley and a stripe-headed tanager (*now known as the western spindalis*) and greater flamingo

Blackburnian warbler

in the Everglades. In Newfoundland he added the northern lapwing to his record list; in California, the least storm-petrel.

The young fellow from Beaumont also joins us, and the two men stand side by side, one of America's top birders and a beginner for whom half the local species are new. Neither knows the other, and only we, by chance, know of their very different perspectives. Both watch and marvel at the beauty of a male northern oriole and of a small flock of rose-breasted grosbeaks that drop in out of a rain-filled sky.

With the shower have come more buntings, orioles, tanagers, thrushes, grosbeaks, vireos, and warblers. Several birders see their first male painted bunting, certainly a worthy contestant for the title of most beautiful bird in the world. Another group is trying to locate the rare Cape May warbler that has been seen off and on throughout the day.

Wandering on down the trail, we count fifty binoculars trained on a newly arrived blackburnian warbler in the top of a large pecan tree. Among these observers are Benton Basham, the beginning birder from Beaumont, and the two young boys with the shared binocular. All are delighted with the beauty of so tiny a work of art; all are sharing one of America's fastest-growing hobbies. This, in its

Our Life with Birds

best form, is the joy of birding, and its universality helps to ensure that places like the Houston Audubon Society's High Island sanctuaries will continue to provide a haven for wildlife for future generations as well.

The northern oriole mentioned in this chapter has since regained is original name—Baltimore oriole.

2

Another Tick for the List

Birders take great joy in finding new birds for the very first time, adding these "lifers" to lists of species they have seen. The most treasured list is usually one that contains all the birds seen during the birder's lifetime, hence the term "lifer" or "life bird" for each new discovery. Other ardent listers may also tally species seen in a single year, in each state or country, and even in their own backyards. Visiting a new country, or a new region of the United States, of course, may produce many such discoveries, for each geographic area and each distinctive habitat contain their own avian residents. Some may be abundant and widespread; others may be rare and difficult to find. For the most part, however, the resident species are predictable, and the traveling birder can make plans to search for them.

In order to build a substantial life list, the ardent birder may also chase rarities that turn up unexpectedly. Such vagrants may be tropical species that occasionally range northward into the United States, refugees from the far North that drift southward on cold Arctic blasts, or oceanic birds blown inland by hurricanes or other storms at sea. Once discovered, these vagrants normally draw huge crowds of birders, some coming from considerable distances. A very rare bird, perhaps sighted for the first time in a given region, may draw hundreds and even thousands of eager watchers, for the sport is growing rapidly, and many birders now have the time and resources to chase these lifers across the continent.

*Although we have never carried birding to these extremes, prefer-
ring to visit a region for a longer period of time and to enjoy as many
of its residents as possible, we nonetheless chase an occasional rarity
that turns up nearby. Sometimes the individual bird remains in one
location and is easy to find, a "stakeout" in birders' parlance. Often,
however, the bird ranges over a wider area, and the pursuit then becomes a search for the proverbial needle in a haystack. These are a few
of the life birds we have sought and found successfully through the
years and subsequently have written about in our columns.*

A Ghost from the Arctic—Snowy Owl: 1977

It is, we think, the most magnificent bird we have ever seen, although
admittedly it is hard to be objective, for this is also a bird that has
eluded us for years. We have hunted for it in the numbing cold of
northern Minnesota winters, and we have waded through snowdrifts
in New York with no success. Now we are finally face-to-face with
this ghost from the Arctic, the snowy owl, and it is perched on, of
all places, a boat dock in Louisiana.

This huge white bird first appeared at the lakeshore home of Mr.
and Mrs. B. A. Holland in Shreveport on December 6, 1976, report-
edly the first snowy owl documented for Louisiana. During the next
few weeks, dozens of bird-watchers came not only from Louisiana
but from across Texas and other neighboring states to see it.

Ironically, we were in Minnesota celebrating a family Christmas
when the owl was first reported on the Houston Rare Bird Alert, a
chain telephone call that keeps birders informed of new ornithological developments. Only after we had been back for some time
did someone remark offhandedly about "the owl" in Shreveport, and
we quickly made weekend plans to set off in hot pursuit.

Fortunately, this unusual visitor decided to stay throughout the
winter, seemingly enjoying a rare storm that dumped several inches
of snow on its adopted neighborhood. The white stuff was undoubtedly more familiar to the owl than to the other residents of Shreveport. How long will it remain? No one knows, but it could be late

spring before it leaves for its Arctic home more than two thousand miles away.

Snowy owl

Circumpolar, the snowy owl is found in Europe and Asia as well as at the northern limits of the North American continent. Its summer home is on the tundra, beyond the tree line and up to the edge of perpetual ice and snow. There it nests on the ground, usually choosing a small hillock where melting snow will not flood the shallow, unlined depression the female scrapes in the earth.

From three to seven nearly round, white eggs constitute a normal clutch, but as many as thirteen have been found. When food is plentiful, the female lays more eggs; when food is scarce, the birds compensate by producing fewer young. Indeed, in times when prey is unavailable, snowy owls may not nest at all. Perhaps there is a lesson here for people, too.

It takes nearly five weeks for the eggs to hatch, and because they are laid at intervals and incubation begins immediately, the downy gray chicks vary greatly in age. The female may be tending some that are nearly grown while still incubating the last of her clutch. Most of the nest chores are handled by the female while the hunting male brings food for her and the chicks. Lemmings and other rodents are the staples of the snowy owl's diet, with Arctic hares, ptarmigan, and other small mammals and birds adding variety.

Beautifully adapted for this land of ice and snow, the owls endure the Arctic winter as long as food is plentiful. Every few years, however, massive rodent die-offs due to stress and disease occur. To survive these periodic "lemming crashes," the snowy owls move southward, sometimes in substantial numbers. During the winter of 1926–27, more than twenty-three hundred birds were recorded in the United States, with Michigan and Maine having more than six hundred each. Although most of these migrant owls remain in the northern tier of states, a few range much farther south. Some have even wandered hundreds of miles out to sea to land on passing ships.

Several snowy owls have wintered in Texas, but none in recent years. Most reports of "white owls" are undoubtedly due to sightings of barn owls by inexperienced birders, for these common birds appear ghostly white when seen in floodlights or car headlights.

The snowy is a diurnal, or day-flying, owl. On its rare southern excursions, it will eat almost anything it can catch and may even feed on carrion. Several reports have described a bird perching at the edge of the water and catching fish in its sharp talons. Shreveport's owl, we have been told, particularly enjoys plump ducks, coots, and tender meadowlarks. It even displayed an interest in a neighborhood cat that brazenly ventured out onto the dock.

As we sit quietly on the lakeshore to sketch and photograph this bird, we are impressed first by its enormous size. We cannot, of course, measure our white prize, but the field guides we carry tell us that snowy owls stand two feet tall and have a five-foot wingspread. When it flies briefly out over the water with strong, deliberate wing beats and then returns to its perch, it seems impossibly large in the fading afternoon light.

Many accounts emphasize the inordinate tameness of the snowy owl, but this bird is uncharacteristically wary. From about seventy-five yards away, we watch it through a spotting scope, gazing into a huge pair of gleaming yellow eyes. It is always tempting to anthropomorphize with owls, but those eyes do, indeed, have a look of haughty indifference that befits so magnificent a creature.

The feathers are creamy white with dark markings near the tips. There are distinct but narrow dark bars across the forehead and only faint barring on the breast. This is perhaps a young male bird, for adult males are more immaculate in plumage, and females have heavier, more pronounced markings. The head is huge and rounded, lacking the "ear" tufts seen on many of our more common owls.

Walking around on the dock from time to time, the bird has a distinct waddle that adds a bit of comic relief. But as it sits stoically, glaring back at us, it is obviously aware of our presence and secure in its lakeside perch. Only the tip of its hooked black beak and long curving talons peep out from beneath the thickly layered white feathers that cover even the toes, shrouding this Arctic ghost in elegance and mystery. The sight is worth every moment of the long, five-hundred-mile drive to add this elusive raptor to our lists.

We have subsequently seen other snowy owls, including some in their more normal habitat along the shores of Hudson Bay in Canada while on a November pursuit of polar bears. On that same trip, we observed several more of the great white owls perched atop runway markers as we rolled down the airport runway in Winnipeg. All were magnificent birds, but none quite equaled that first unprecedented lifer added to our lists in Louisiana.

Tiny Nomads from Mexico—Golden-crowned Warbler and Tropical Parula: 1980

It is not a particularly striking bird. No more than five inches long, the golden-crowned warbler is olive gray above and yellow below, the golden crown stripe that gives it its name bordered broadly in black. Yet this rather shy little warbler has been causing quite a furor among bird-watchers. From around the country, they have been flocking to Texas to see a species not normally encountered north of the Rio Grande.

The now-famous visitor from across the border has taken up temporary residence at the home of Mr. and Mrs. Sydney Benn in Brownsville. The Benn yard is always a popular stop for birders, for here may be found many of the subtropical species for which the Rio Grande Valley is noted. Green jays and white-fronted doves *(now white-tipped doves)* come to seed scattered on the ground, and noisy chachalacas nibble greens in the garden. Feeders attract several buff-bellied hummingbirds throughout the year, and colorful orioles and lingering warblers ornament the fruit trees.

This golden-crowned warbler was first discovered by Jeri Langham on December 29, 1979. A biology professor at California State University, Sacramento, Langham was on a birding vacation in Texas and stopped to see the hummingbirds and other resident species. He did not dream he would trigger a winter migration of bird-watchers through the Benns' backyard.

Resident in hillside forests of Mexico, ranging southward through Central and South America to Argentina, the golden-crowned warbler has been seen only once before in the United States. This was a sighting by well-known ornithologist Irby Davis near Harlingen in 1945. *The Bird Life of Texas* by Harry Oberholser cites two other specimens collected at Brownsville in 1892; however, some question the authenticity of those records.

Thus, the little bird discovered by Langham is the first North American record in thirty-five years, and repeated sightings and subsequent photographs provide the only unequivocal documentation of the species' occurrence across the Rio Grande. Small wonder that the news spread rapidly throughout the birding fraternity.

On a trip to the Valley in late January, we learned that the war-

Golden-crowned warbler

bler was still being seen, and we, too, found ourselves on the Benns' doorstep. Rather than being annoyed at yet more birders in dirty boots, Mr. and Mrs. Benn seemed delighted to invite us in and show us where the bird had most frequently been seen. They derive a great deal of pleasure from their birds and enjoy showing them to others.

We began optimistically by scanning the trees in the backyard, a yard Sydney Benn describes as "good for birds, not for growing grass," and then scoured the shrub-bordered alley behind. We found numerous wrens and thrashers, a wintering redstart, and a Nashville warbler, but no golden-crowned warbler. Again we retraced our steps without success.

Moving down into the brushy woods bordering a resaca, we crawled through tangles of vines and squirmed through the bushes, leaving deep footprints in the mud and patches of skin on the abundant thorns. Again no luck. An hour passed; then two. We had a schedule to keep, but we did not want to leave without finding what was probably the only golden-crowned warbler we would ever see in North America.

About noon, we found two pretty little birds with bluish heads, greenish backs, and yellow breasts. Their faces sported distinct black masks, a diagnostic mark of the tropical parula warbler, a species we had sought before with no success. This was a new bird for our U.S. list, and we were elated, but it was not THE warbler. Determinedly, we covered the circuit again.

After four hours, success came with surprising ease. Suddenly, in a bush in front of us, we spotted an olive-and-yellow bird, so close we could not focus binoculars on it. As it turned its head, we could clearly see the black-bordered golden crown. Here it was, after all our searching, no more than five feet away. It stared back at us for several minutes before moving quietly away through the thicket.

Signing the Benns' register of visitors, we counted more than seventy people who had come to see the golden-crowned warbler. Some were from Houston and other Texas cities, but the addresses included Indiana, Illinois, Minnesota, Michigan, Tennessee, and Oklahoma. There were names from Colorado, Arizona, Florida, Maryland, Connecticut, Kentucky, and South Carolina.

Paul DuMont, currently the leader in number of birds seen in North America, came from Washington, D.C., to add number 727 to his list. Renowned tour leader and bird-book author Ben King wrote a large "#701" beside his signature. As a friend of ours noted, with less reverence than some would think appropriate, "All the birdie biggies had joined the migration to Brownsville."

To many, we are sure, such furor over a single tiny bird is inexplicable. In sober reflection, we are sometimes inclined to agree. Yet ardent birders delight in the game of adding to their lists. And even more, they delight in seeing something new. The latter, we believe, is a worthy driving force in life.

We would find several more tropical parulas in subsequent years while visiting such Rio Grande Valley "hot spots" as Santa Ana National Wildlife Refuge and Anzalduas County Park. However, it was not until November 12, 2002, nearly twenty-three years later, that we would again see a golden-crowned warbler north of the Rio Grande.

While attending the Rio Grande Valley Birding Festival in Harlingen, we learned of a golden-crown discovered by Dr. Tim Brush on November 2 on the campus of the University of Texas/Pan American in Edinburg. The bird remained for many days, frequenting a huge tropical fig and a group of surrounding trees, and provided a focal point for many festival field trips. It was there that we, too, would find it after a lengthy search, perched overhead in a large live oak, calmly preening the yellow feathers of its breast and occasionally pausing to peer down at us. What a treat to see once again this tiny nomad from Mexico that had led us a merry chase almost a quarter century ago.

Avian Invaders—Brown Jay: 1981

It is a warm but cloudy morning as we emerge from the dense mesquite thicket to stand on the northern bank of the Rio Grande. A small flock of green jays, purple-and-black heads contrasting brilliantly with green-and-yellow body plumage, noisily announces our presence. Slowly we work our way downstream, checking off on a mental list the other subtropical birds we see in this birder's paradise along the Mexican border.

"Listen for a red-shouldered hawk," Houston birder Ted Eubanks had told us, but the morning goes by with no such call. We begin to despair of finding our quarry.

Then, far in the distance, we hear a repeated scream, *kee-yer, kee-yer,* and we quicken our pace to locate the source, working our way around eroded gullies and following meandering cattle trails through the brush. Finally, in the top of a huge riverside willow, we spot a large bird, and it screams again. It is, indeed, a hawk. We stop in disappointment, for we had been searching not for the red-shouldered hawk itself but for another species that commonly mimics it, as do the blue jays in East Texas.

Conscious of our approach, the hawk takes wing, and at the same time there is a raucous chorus from the thicket beneath its perch. *Thief, thief, thief.* The cries are much like those of the blue jay, but hoarser and seemingly louder. Our spirits rise again.

We creep forward, and from around a branch peers another large bird, one with a very long tail and dark, sooty brown plumage shading to whitish beneath. Through our binoculars we see a bright yellow bill and a startling yellow eye ring.

This is the bird we have come to find, a species that is not pictured in the common field guides of U.S. birds (*it has subsequently been added*). It warrants no mention in *Birds of North America* by Chandler Robbins and his coauthors, nor is it included in *A Field Guide to the Birds of Texas* by Roger Tory Peterson. For this is a Mexican brown jay, a relative newcomer to the Texas side of the Rio Grande.

The first sightings of this new invader (each sighting was of two individuals) given credence by Harry Oberholser were reported in 1969 and 1972 along the river below Falcon Dam. Then, in 1974, a small flock of brown jays was discovered on the Santa Margarita Ranch, also a short distance below the massive dam. A nest was later discovered, providing evidence of the first breeding of the species within the state. Word spread among birders, and frequent visitors to Santa

Margarita Ranch found other rarities as well. Soon it became known as one of the "hot spots" of birding in the Rio Grande Valley.

We have searched here before for the brown jay, but without success. Now, as we stand looking at our first Texas specimen, we are surprised at how big and beautiful it seems. Farther south in Mexico, where this jay is common, it has always seemed to be a pest that taunts the birder wandering through the forests, alerting other birds to the birder's presence. Here, it is a rare prize and thus seems somehow more striking and noble.

The yellow beak and eye ring, too, give this individual a special attraction. These are the marks of an immature bird and will disappear with age, the bill turning black in the coming season. Indeed, another jay now makes its appearance, and this one has the dark bill of an adult. Then another takes wing from a low branch, and the others join it, disappearing through the trees with a noisy warning, *thief, thief.*

Early in the afternoon, as we sit quietly on the riverbank, watching the shallow Rio Grande ripple over a gravel bar, we again hear the persistent cry. This time, eight jays stream into the tree above us, hopping about and peering down at us for a few moments before trooping off again in pursuit of a more worthy subject of their jeers. Later we spot two more upriver at Chapeño, an exciting total of thirteen for our first sightings of Texas brown jays.

This fascinating bird, nearly as large as a crow, normally makes its home in eastern Mexico and thence southward along the Caribbean slope to Panama. Now it has pushed northward, apparently to stay, where it has found the mesquite scrub forests and large willows bordering the river to be similar to its native habitat.

Searching for the jays here, bird-watchers also find other equally rare species to add to the growing list of Texas birds. The hook-billed kite, clay-colored and rufous-backed robins, golden-crowned warbler, gray hawk, ringed kingfisher, and many more are avian prizes to be sought along the banks of the Rio Grande. Hopefully, the few remaining patches of thorn-scrub woodland will always be preserved so that South Texas will continue to provide a haven for tropical species found nowhere else in the United States.

Immature brown jay

Efforts continue to preserve the remnant woodlands along the Rio Grande and to acquire and reforest additional tracts. The brown jay and the ringed kingfisher have increased their numbers along the river and are no longer the rarities they were a few decades ago. Although by no means common, they can usually be found by the dedicated birder.

A New Texas Gull—Black-headed Gull: 1982

It has not been a particularly good winter for birds, especially for the rarities so eagerly sought. During the first week of the new year, however, a report of a very rare species caused a great deal of excitement among local Houston birders. A black-headed gull, the first ever reported in the state, was found on Lake Livingston in Polk County, far from its normal European haunts.

The black-headed is one of the more common gulls of Europe, ranging across the northern portions of that continent and Asia and wintering southward into Africa. It has also become a rare but regular winter visitor to the shores of northeastern North America. Although its presence might be expected along the coast of Maine or Massachusetts, it has never, to our knowledge, been seen in Texas.

This unusual visitor was sighted by Kelly Bryan and Tony Gallucci during a Christmas Count on Lake Livingston on January 2, 1982. Both experienced ornithologists, they had already spotted a rare black-legged kittiwake and some laughing gulls among the immense mixed flock of gulls and terns feeding at the outfall of the dam. Laughing gulls, too, are unusual away from the salt water of the coast.

Scanning a flock of nearly four thousand Bonaparte's gulls sitting on the water above the dam, they discovered a slightly larger bird with the same general coloration and pattern. It had, however, a red bill that contrasted with the black bills of its companions. Here, Bryan and Gallucci realized, was something new. Having just examined the pictures of rare gulls in the field guides, they immediately identified it as a black-headed gull.

Called by Gallucci that afternoon, we put out the report on the area Rare Bird Alert, and by the time we could reach the lake early the following morning, other birders were already there.

From the top of the embankment, we used spotting scopes to examine each of the thousands of gulls bobbing in the rough water. Below the dam, hundreds of others wheeled and circled above the raging current, catching small fish amid the boats of their human counterparts. It seemed almost hopeless, the proverbial but constantly moving needle in a very large aquatic haystack.

We found the kittiwake without much difficulty, a handsome and distinctively marked gull from the far North. It had the characteristic wing pattern, band across the nape of the neck, and slightly forked tail with black border of an immature bird. Of the dozen or so kittiwakes we have seen in Texas, all have been immatures. They seem more inclined than established adults to wander.

Suddenly Linda Roach, Houston artist and bird-tour leader (*now Linda Feltner of Seattle, Washington*), shouted that she had located a suspicious-looking gull. We rushed to her side and quickly picked up the bird from her description. A half-dozen binoculars followed the single gull as it alternately soared high into the sky and swooped low over the surface of the water.

It was, indeed, larger than the nearby Bonaparte's gulls, which it resembled, and the upper back and wing surfaces appeared a paler pearly gray. This is a characteristic not mentioned in most of the guides, but it proved to be useful in spotting the bird among hundreds of others. The wing tips bore the white wedge-shaped markings of the Bonaparte's, but as our bird circled, we could see that the primaries were dark below, a diagnostic mark.

Black-headed gull
in winter plumage

They were, in fact, much blacker than we had expected from field-guide illustrations. In spite of its name, there was no dark head, for that plumage is characteristic only in the breeding season; in winter, there is only a dark spot behind the eye. As it flew closer, we could see the red legs and the bloodred bill. There was no question; all the key field marks were there. This was a black-headed gull. We were seeing the first one ever reported in Texas.

For long periods of time we lost sight of our European visitor, only to spot it again for a minute or two as it soared past in buoyant flight. Attempts to photograph it were less than successful, but there are probably pictures of sufficient quality to document the bird's appearance.

It is hard to explain the excitement generated by a single small gull spotted by two patient, sharp-eyed expert birders. Yet throughout the day, others arrived from Houston, from Beaumont, and from cities across the area. Some came to add the species to already-lengthy lists; others, perhaps, came simply out of curiosity. All saw something new and interesting, reason enough for all the excitement.

The Wandering Cuckoo—Mangrove Cuckoo: 1982

Yet another new bird species has been added to the Texas list in the early days of 1982. We have written about the first black-headed gull to be seen within the boundaries of the state; at about the same time, a rare mangrove cuckoo was also causing a furor among local birders. It had taken up temporary residence near the Bolivar ferry landing and was seen by many from the Houston area.

As its name indicates, the mangrove cuckoo is primarily an inhabitant of low mangrove thickets along the coast. In the United States, it is confined to the Florida Keys and the adjacent peninsula as far north as Tampa Bay. It also occurs in the West Indies and through tropical America, from coastal Mexico and the Yucatán to northern Brazil.

Even within its normal range, it is not an easy bird to find. One author describes it as a very shy cuckoo that "darts straight for a tangled mangrove swamp when disturbed." The Audubon Society *Field Guide to North American Birds* calls it "difficult to observe, remaining hidden in dense thickets much of the time."

The mangrove cuckoo is a slender, foot-long bird about the size of a blue jay, with a loose-jointed, graduated tail. It resembles the yellow-billed cuckoo, sometimes popularly called the "rain crow," that is common in our area. It differs, however, in having buff underparts instead of white and a black mask through the eyes. Older field guides called it the "black-eared cuckoo" because of the latter characteristic.

The unusual wanderer was first spotted, we are told, on the day of New Year's Eve, and appropriately enough, its discoverers were also visitors from out of state. A birder named Eugene Armstrong from Booneville, Iowa, and a nature-tour group from Arkansas were both waiting in line on the Bolivar side for the Galveston ferry. Independently, they noticed the cuckoo sitting in a thicket beside the road and realized its rarity. Both called David Dauphin in Baytown to start the Rare Bird Alert. The first local birders to appear on the scene, however, did not find the bird, and interest waned for several days. Then it was seen again in the same spot, and the bird-watcher migration to Bolivar began.

On January 6, Jim Morgan called us to say that he had just seen and photographed the bird; an hour and a half later, we were there. Instructions were simple: park on the shoulder of the road by the green sign, and watch for the cuckoo in the rattle-bean bushes across the ditch. It had also been seen perching on the barbed-wire fence.

We watched and waited patiently, scanning the bushes and the fence line again and again. Not a bird moved anywhere. Houstonians Margaret Anderson and Ellen Red were also on the scene, and we took comfort in the added pairs of watchful eyes. We studied the field guides so we would be prepared. Nothing. Another hour passed. Still no sign of any cuckoo.

Less patient now, we tramped through the thicket, part of it knee-deep in water. Then John wandered through the adjoining brushy field while Gloria prowled along the road. No luck there. Just as we were heading for some distant thickets, Margaret Anderson appeared on the road, waving her arms wildly. The message was all too clear; we should have been more patient.

Running, panting, stumbling—through the water and under the fence. Had anyone observed us, we would certainly have reaffirmed

Mangrove cuckoo

a long-held opinion of bird-watchers. Reaching the road, we followed Margaret's pointing finger. There sat our first mangrove cuckoo—right beside the green sign.

There could be no doubt about this bird. The breast was much brighter than many of the books indicate, a rich yellow buff shading almost to orange beneath the wings. The bill was long and decurved; the eyes surrounded by brilliant yellow rings. The black mask was the clincher.

Slowly and quietly the cuckoo moved through the thicket of sedges and rattle bean, the closest thing to its normal habitat with not a mangrove in sight. It ate a caterpillar and a moth and quietly watched us as we stared back at it. Our photographs and quick field sketches can never convey its beauty. We were elated. With the black-headed gull, this was our second new bird in four days.

It should be noted that there is one other "sight record" of a mangrove cuckoo along the Texas coast. Interestingly enough, this was in Galveston at about the same time of year, a Christmas Count on December 30, 1964. The three observers were certainly credible, but the bird was not seen again. The lack of photos and other evidence necessitated calling it a "hypothetical" sighting.

Our current bird, however, has been seen by dozens, perhaps hundreds, of birders and photographed in color by several of them. It will now go into the ornithological records as the first official mangrove cuckoo in Texas.

Rarities from Two Continents—Curlew Sandpiper and Yucatan Vireo: 1984

It is not uncommon for the Houston-Galveston area to shelter rare bird species, especially during the migration season, for the Texas coast is a virtual crossroads for avian wanderers. April 1984, however, was particularly exciting for area birders, with two extremely unusual birds being discovered on the Bolivar Peninsula. One of those sightings constituted the first record of the species for the United States.

On Saturday, April 28, visiting Swedish bird artist and author Lars Jonsson was looking over the shorebirds in a marsh near Crystal Beach. With the dunlins, dowitchers, and other sandpipers was one he recognized as a curlew sandpiper. Jonsson's intimate familiarity with European birds was extremely helpful in identifying the very rare visitor that has been seen only once previously on the upper Texas coast. That earlier sighting was many years ago and was not documented by photographs as this newest record has been.

The curlew sandpiper breeds on the Arctic tundra of Siberia and winters in southern Eurasia and Africa; in migration it ranges across Europe. As might be expected, it is encountered most often in North America as a wayward straggler along the northeastern Atlantic coast, although it also breeds occasionally in Alaska. Although not without precedent, its presence in Texas caused a flurry within the birding fraternity, few of whom had ever seen the species before.

Within hours, word of the discovery had spread up and down the coast, for most area birders congregate in Galveston, High Island, and Bolivar on weekends during April and May, the peak of spring migration. By afternoon, between fifty and sixty people had added the curlew sandpiper to their lists, and others were on their way from throughout the state. This was an ornithological find of major importance, but it was soon to be eclipsed by a still more unexpected one.

On Sunday, while literally hundreds of people with binoculars and spotting scopes lined the little gravel road known to birders as Bob's Bait Camp Road to watch the sandpiper, four others were searching a small wooded area on the Sun Oil Company lease a short distance up the Bolivar Peninsula. Here, Jim Morgan, Ted and Virginia Eubanks, and Larry White discovered another bird that they immediately recognized as something different.

Obviously a vireo, it was unusually large for a member of that family, and its bill was even longer and more massive than those of the common Texas vireos. The head and upperparts were drab brown, with a prominent dusky eyebrow stripe. The underparts were brownish gray tinged with yellow.

Fortunately for science and for area birders, the strange vireo was captured in a bird-banding net, and the quartet of experienced and careful birders photographed it in the hand and took detailed measurements and notes before it was released. With these data, they began a search of the literature, discarding the more common vireos that did not fit their observations and finally deciding it could be nothing but a Yucatan vireo, a bird never before seen north of Mexico.

So careful was the documentation, in fact, that it seems likely the bird can be considered a female of the Cozumel race of the Yucatan vireo. With the measurements and photographs, there can be little doubt it will be accepted by ornithologists as a new North American record. Experts familiar with tropical birds have subsequently seen this individual and concur in the identification.

Thus it was that we arrived on the Bolivar Peninsula in hopes of adding two new birds to our life list of species seen in the United States. We were very late because of other commitments. Most area birders had already seen the sandpiper; many were now in search of the vireo. We hoped we were not too late.

The little marsh along the bait-camp road held a multitude of shorebirds, poking and probing in the mud for the myriad invertebrates that fuel their migratory flights. With a group of dunlins was another sandpiper of about the same body size, but with longer legs and neck, giving it a much lankier look. It lacked the black patch on the belly the dunlins were developing in their spring plumage, and the bill curved downward uniformly through its entire length rather than drooped at the tip as does the bill of the dunlin. It had to be a curlew sandpiper! A lifer!

On up the road, we headed into the little motte of trees on the Sun Oil lease near Gilchrist. Thanks to Sun and the Wiggins family that owns the land, access had been permitted to the area where the vireo had been found. We had been told it was frequenting a particular tree the day before, feeding on insects attracted to the fresh blossoms of a Hercules-club, or toothache tree. No sooner had we parked than there it was, and it allowed us within a few feet to study every detail. This was almost too easy, for here was a species never before seen in the United States. A second lifer in less than an hour.

Our Life with Birds

Over the past few months we have explored such wonderful places as Costa Rica and Puerto Rico, observing tropical birds of incredible beauty. Perhaps no other birds have been as exciting, however, as the curlew sandpiper and the Yucatan vireo right here at home. From the rush to the coast, it is obvious that other bird-watchers share our enthusiasm.

Yucatan vireo

A Strange Flycatcher—Greenish Elaenia: 1984

It is early on a rainy Monday morning in late May when the telephone awakens us from a deep sleep. Groggy, John reaches for it and mutters a less-than-cordial greeting. With the first sentence, however, he is wide awake, and the thought of more sleep for either of us is banished immediately. Another very rare bird has been found on the Texas coast.

The caller is Margaret Anderson, a longtime friend and one of Houston's finest birders. She is on her way to High Island, where a greenish elaenia, a Mexican member of the flycatcher family, has been seen the day before. Within minutes we, too, are headed for that little coastal town to join a converging stream of bird-watchers.

Certainly this has been a record-setting spring for rare birds in the Houston-Galveston area. We had written recently about the curlew sandpiper and the Yucatan vireo, the latter a new North American record, that were found on the Bolivar Peninsula only a few miles apart. Nearly a thousand birders from across the country came to see the vireo, which stayed for several days in the small patch of trees. A European little gull was also found and photographed near San Luis Pass, and several other unusual species were spotted in migration along the coast.

Ordinarily, we would be skeptical of the report of the elaenia, for this, too, would be a North American record, the first time the species had been seen north of Mexico. It is not an exceptionally distinctive bird nor an easy one to identify, and there are hundreds of species of flycatchers that range across the New World, some so similarly marked that they are best identified by song. But the identification in this case seemed certain; the bird, like the Yucatan vireo before it, had been captured and carefully examined before releasing it again.

Amazingly, one of the same people, Houston's Jim Morgan, was also involved in the discovery of this new bird. On Sunday, May 20, Morgan and Linda Feltner, a wildlife artist and tour leader, were combing the thickets for warblers at the Louis Smith Bird Sanctuary in High Island. Recently purchased by the Houston Audubon Society, the sanctuary is an important haven for birds migrating along our Texas coast.

Seeing a small bird with a yellow belly and dark upperparts, they expected a warbler, perhaps even one of the genus that includes the Connecticut and MacGillivray's warblers, uncommon species in our area. But the tail was too long, and the shape and actions of this bird were all wrong. "It was obviously a flycatcher," said Morgan, "but it didn't look like any North American species I could think of." He took some photographs, and Feltner began to sketch the mystery bird.

"If I were in Mexico, I'd call it a greenish elaenia," Morgan remarked, for it seemed to fit all the field marks—bright yellow belly, gray chest, olive green upperparts. A key factor appeared to be the absence of wing bars, markings that are present on many elaenias and other flycatchers. There should be a yellow patch on the crown, but that is often concealed and not detectable in the field.

Carefully, Morgan and Feltner sorted through and discarded other possibilities for the bird's identity. They now had tentatively decided it must be the rare elaenia, improbable as that seemed.

"I thought we might have a good chance to net it," says Morgan, and he called Ted Eubanks and Ron Braun, who arrived that afternoon with their large bird-banding mist nets.

With nets strung through the woods, they kept away to avoid chasing the flycatcher higher into the treetops. And it worked. A little more than an hour later, at 4:05 P.M., the bird was in the net. In the hand, the yellow patch on the head was clearly visible. There were no wing bars.

Greenish elaenia

The greenish elaenia had been added to the list of U.S. birds. It was carefully measured, weighed, and photographed in great detail, and those measurements subsequently agreed well with published data for the species. It was then banded and released.

Thus it is that we join the rush to High Island the following morning. The elaenia will be hard to find, for it frequents thickets and low growth, unlike most of its flycatcher relatives. We know, however, that we will not be searching alone, and indeed, there are several other birders already there when we arrive.

Gary Clark finally spots our quarry, and we creep toward it through the underbrush when Gary calls. At first we cannot find the bird, and we search frantically, afraid it will fly again before we see it. Finally, there it is, perched low on a grapevine; we had been looking too far away. Yellow belly, gray chest, dark olive back, no wing bars—our first greenish elaenia. The first one ever seen in the United States.

As we leave the woods, elated, others arrive to begin their quest. Surely the following days will bring hundreds of birders to High Island in search of their first elaenia. To the uninitiated, it seems a great deal of furor for a single six-inch bird, but to the ardent birder, it is one of the most exciting of events.

The Wayward Duck—Barrow's Goldeneye: 1991

The beautiful black-and-white duck swims contentedly on the small pond, diving repeatedly for food. Its bright pattern marks it unmistakably as a male Barrow's goldeneye, a species John has seen but twice before, in Alaska and in Yellowstone National Park. This bird is especially exciting, however, because it provides only the second verified record for Texas and is one that Gloria has never seen.

Instead of swimming through the wave-lashed inlets of the Alaskan coast or in the icy waters of a Rocky Mountain lake rimmed by lodgepole pines, it frolics against a backdrop of chemical units and processing towers. For some unknown reason, it has wandered far off its normal route and has taken up residence at Occidental Chemical Corporation's Battleground Plant within sight of the San Jacinto Monument east of Houston.

The wayward duck was first discovered in late December by OxyChem process operator Leon Lalonde, who is also an ardent birder. Realizing it was extremely rare, Lalonde showed it to fellow employee and birder Buddy Hollis. Together they pored over the field guides and verified its identity as a Barrow's goldeneye.

The sighting was reported to the Houston Audubon Society's Texas Rare Bird Alert, a recorded telephone message that details unusual reports from around the state, and birders flocked to see it. When we first learned of it two days later, we had been preceded by about 40 others. By the end of the first weekend, the total exceeded 150 visitors from as far away as Nacogdoches, Waco, and Austin. For most, it was a new bird on their lifetime lists; for all, it was the first such encounter within the borders of the state.

The first Barrow's goldeneye officially recorded for Texas was shot by a hunter near Greenville in Hunt County on November 6, 1958. It was verified by the Dallas Museum of Natural History and later mounted. A few other sightings were reported in Chambers and

Our Life with Birds

Aransas Counties during the 1950s, but none could be substantiated. The Texas Bird Records Committee requires documentation by specimen, photos, or tape recordings of a characteristic song in order to establish a first state record. Subsequent encounters with rare birds must be backed up by detailed notes by the observers.

Thus, the present visitor to Battleground Road represents only the second unquestionable occurrence of Barrow's goldeneye in Texas. It has been well photographed, and fortunately it is a male in full breeding plumage. That makes the task of identification much easier. Large white crescents on its dark, purple-glossed head characterize the male, one crescent on each side of the face between the bill and eye. Its black back is spotted with white; its underparts are immaculate white.

A near relative, the common goldeneye, occurs frequently along the Texas coast in winter. However, its greenish head has round facial spots rather than crescents, and the upperparts are more heavily marked with white. Drabber females of the two species are almost identical and present a much more difficult identification problem than do the colorful males.

Barrow's goldeneye has a disjunct breeding range, with one population in the Pacific Northwest and another in Labrador, Greenland, and Iceland. The former winters along the northern Pacific Coast; the latter, from Canada's Gulf of St. Lawrence southward to Maine. It is impossible to say where our present visitor belongs, but it has obviously strayed far from its normal range.

The strip along the Houston Ship Channel is one of the most heavily industrialized areas in the country, and it presents a strange winter home for the Barrow's goldeneye, a bird that should be more at ease along our rocky northern coasts. Nevertheless, the charming little duck seems quite content in this novel environment.

There are, we think, several things to be learned from this experience with so rare a duck. Most obvious is the fact that we can enjoy nature almost everywhere, and new experiences await us around every corner. We will not deny that a trip to Alaska to spot Barrow's goldeneye would be more scenic and aesthetically rewarding, but most of us are not free to make that trip. Even in our everyday urban lives, we can discover rare gems that are ours to enjoy for the moment.

More important, we learn that industry and environmental interests can and must work together. They need not always be adversaries, and both can learn from this experience.

OxyChem has gone out of its way to be a good host to both the Barrow's goldeneye and Texas birders. The company has roped off the long, narrow pond to avoid disturbing the diving duck and constructed a large, elevated platform to provide birders with a better view. Visitors have been surprised and pleased with the friendly reception, and we suspect the company has been surprised by the interest generated by process operator Leon Lalonde's rare discovery.

The pond the duck adopted is part of OxyChem's water-clarification system. Ten million gallons a day of river water are used to cool the processing units, but the water must be freed of suspended sand and other solids before it can be circulated through the plant. Most of that sand settles out in the open ponds, and more is removed by filtration. Only then is the water clean enough to use. It does not come into contact with any petrochemicals and is returned cleaner

Barrow's goldeneye

Our Life with Birds

than it was before, minus a million pounds of sediments every year. These settling ponds teem with fish and crayfish, and it is apparently the latter crustaceans that the goldeneye finds so attractive. It has found a substitute environment that contains some of its favorite foods.

"We are thrilled that people have the opportunity to see this rare bird," said OxyChem plant manager Arthur Lynnworth. He is proud of the plant's record in cutting emissions in half since 1987, largely "by the direct involvement of all our people who are interested in the environment and are trying to do a better job."

Jim Kachtick, OxyChem's environmental manager for the Southern region echoes these sentiments. "We want to maintain a good-neighbor policy to people and to the flora and fauna. We work hard to be a good corporate citizen, and we're trying to do the right things."

"We are impressed with OxyChem's concern for the Barrow's goldeneye and with their efforts to help birders have this once-in-a-lifetime experience," says Sandra Hoover, executive director of the Houston Audubon Society. "They have gone out of their way to be gracious."

Perhaps this one small but colorful duck can help both sides in a sometimes contentious debate realize that people really do care about the fate of the environment. If so, it has provided not only a unique birding experience but a worthwhile conservation lesson during its unprecedented wanderings to a strange new habitat.

Treasure on a Galveston Beach—Kelp Gull: 1996

The large gull is easy to spot as it stands quietly on the beach near the base of the Galveston jetty. About the size of a nearby herring gull, it towers over the resident laughing gulls, black skimmers, and several species of terns with which it shares the sand and surf. Most striking, however, are its jet black back and folded wings, contrasting with its gleaming white head, neck, tail, and underparts. A handsome bird in the bright sunlight, it has a regal air as it paces the beach, stopping to pick at a catfish lying in the shallow water.

Overjoyed that we have found the bird we seek, we watch from our car as it strides back and forth on the sand. Soon we are joined by other birders who park nearby. Dozens of binoculars track this single bird; smiling faces and nodded greetings reflect the pleasure at the sighting.

Our prize is a kelp gull, the first ever reported in Texas. For most of the assembled throng it is the ultimate lifer, a new bird for their lists. Indeed, although there have been one or two reports of the species along the Gulf Coast in Louisiana and Mississippi, documentation has apparently been lacking. The species has not yet been added to the official roll of North American birds.

The kelp gull, *Larus dominicanus*, is a bird of the Southern Hemisphere. Also called the southern black-backed gull or Dominican gull, it breeds along the South American coast, from southeastern Brazil around Tierra del Fuego to Peru, sometimes wandering well inland in the Andes. Other races of the species inhabit southern Africa, Australia and New Zealand, and a host of islands in the surrounding seas. The kelp gull also abounds on the Antarctic Peninsula, one of the few gulls to breed in the Antarctic and Subantarctic zones.

In spite of its circumpolar range in the Southern Hemisphere, the kelp gull normally reaches the equator only as a wanderer along the coast of Ecuador. Steve Howell, in his new field guide to Mexican birds, also reports at least two adults on the Yucatán Peninsula during several winters since 1987.

Although we have seen numerous kelp gulls along the South American coasts, we are elated with this sighting in our own backyard. We spend the day with this unprecedented visitor to Texas, shooting pictures, making sketches, and sharing the moment with excited birders from far and wide.

The rare gull has been present in Galveston since at least December 1995; however, it was first misidentified as a great black-backed gull. Although also rare in Texas, the latter species is a wanderer from the far North that occurs occasionally along our coast.

On February 4, 1996, the bird in question was seen by Bob Behrstock and Jon Dunn, two of the foremost bird experts in the country. They quickly realized that although large, it was smaller than the massive great black-backed gull and that it had yellow green legs instead of pink. They further noted at close range the gull's pale ivory yellow eye surrounded by a narrow red orbital ring and its heavy yellow bill tipped with a red spot. There was no pattern of white in the wing tips that marks most other large black gulls, nor was there the dusky streaking on the head displayed by many such birds in winter plumage.

These careful observations ruled out both great and lesser black-backed gulls, the western gull, and the slaty-backed gull, the latter a Siberian species that has strayed on rare occasions through the United States. Barring an improbable hybrid, and plumage characteristics seemed to rule that out, Behrstock and Dunn concluded that the Galveston bird could only be a kelp gull.

Thus it is that we arrive to see this special visitor from the South. We watch throughout a warm, sunlit day as it feeds on fish and a large blue crab washed up along the beach. We note that other gulls do not attempt to steal its catch as they so often do; there is no free-wheeling, screaming chase after each tempting morsel. The kelp gull seems to reign supreme.

Occasionally, it takes wing and circles low overhead, exposing other aspects of its distinctive plumage. We see dusky shading at the tip of a tail feather and heavy molt on the upper surface of the wings. These features, and the absence of a small white spot near the tip of the first primary, indicate that the gull is probably just entering its fourth year, the time at which it gains full adult plumage.

We move with it farther out the jetty and follow it as it joins a group of gulls and terns along the little road down from the seawall toward East Beach. Only as the sun sets behind us do we leave the scene, the kelp gull still standing proudly on the patch of sand that it has claimed.

Kelp gull

Galveston birder Fae Humphrey reports that nearly a thousand people came to see the gull on the first weekend after its identification by Dunn and Behrstock. Monitoring the scene, Humphrey logged in birders from nineteen states and Canada, all intent on adding the kelp gull to their lists.

Faced with Galveston's Mardi Gras celebration, Island officials had intended to close the jetty beach to vehicles; however, they relented when told about the gull and its horde of potential visitors. Posting a guard, they graciously allowed access to this avian treasure, earning the gratitude of birders from across the continent.

Joining the kelp gull from time to time have been an adult lesser black-backed gull and immature great black-backed and glaucous gulls, all rare wanderers to the Texas coast. They have combined to make the Galveston beach one of the most famous in the country.

A few kelp gulls have nested in recent years on the Chandeleur Islands off southeastern Louisiana, occasionally pairing with herring gulls to produce hybrids. The possibility of such a hybrid has been suggested for the 1996 Galveston bird; however, the Texas Bird Records Committee officially added the kelp gull to the state list.

An Arctic Eider Comes to Texas—King Eider: 1998

A spectacular duck has staged a surprise visit to Texas and is making waves throughout the birding community. Finding a temporary refuge on Quintana Beach in Brazoria County, a king eider swims and dives in the rolling surf or rests quietly on the sandy beach. What makes the eider's appearance so exciting for area birders is the fact that the species seldom ranges south from the high Arctic. It will apparently go down in ornithological history as the first documented king eider within the boundaries of our state.

While attending the 1998 Brazosport Migration Celebration, the fourth such annual event, we began to hear reports of this rare visitor. Members of a team participating in the week-long Great Texas Birding Classic had spotted it near Quintana County Park on April 30, and we later learned that fishermen had been seeing the "funny-looking bird" for at least two weeks.

On the beach early the next morning, we finally located the bird far out in the surf, but strong winds and breaking waves made observation extremely difficult. The duck dove repeatedly and remained on the surface for only a few seconds at a time. The profile seemed to fit that of an eider, and at times we thought we could get a glimpse of an orange bill and white patches in its facial plumage. The back of the duck was dark; its chest and neck, light. There seemed to be a narrow dark collar around its neck.

Some of this fit with the descriptions of an immature male king eider, but we were far from secure in our identification. The books we had available did not show the molt sequences and various immature plumages. And although we had seen eiders in Greenland and Arctic Canada the previous summer, this strange bird resembled those only in its large, bulky size and the profile of its head and beak.

Indeed, there are discrepancies even among standard reference guides. The National Geographic field guide used by many birders says of the male king eider: "Full adult plumage is attained by fourth winter." Steve Madge and Hilary Burn in *Waterfowl*, however, write that the male attains fully adult plumage by its third winter.

This Texas eider was first described in reports we heard as a "first-winter male," but it certainly has more light markings than field-guide illustrations of that plumage. The current tape recording on the Texas Rare Bird Alert calls it a "third-year male," and other opinions will undoubtedly surface.

We left Quintana Beach last Friday morning less than secure in our sighting of a king eider. Clearly, photographic documentation would be vital in establishing the true identity of the mystery bird.

Harry Oberholser, in his monumental work *The Bird Life of Texas,* cites a single Texas record for the king eider and lists the species as "hypothetical" within the state. He describes "one careful sighting" by Dr. Leonard Goldman and legendary Texas birder Connie Hagar of a male in breeding plumage on the Rockport beach on October 23, 1968. "The bird," wrote Oberholser, "was sitting on the beach when sighted and allowed approach to within a few feet before sliding into the water."

Such sight records of highly unusual birds, however, are not normally accepted as fact, especially when they are of a bird far out of its typical range and never before seen within the state. New birds are added to the state list only when fully documented. Thus, the third edition of the *Checklist of the Birds of Texas* published by the Texas Ornithological Society in 1995 lists the king eider as a "non-accepted species," although it notes Oberholser's report of the Rockport bird.

The reasons for skepticism are obvious. Although common on the Arctic tundra of northern Alaska and Canada, as well as in such remote locations as Greenland and Siberia, the king eider rarely ventures far southward. Madge and Burn write that it "lives only marginally south of the Arctic Circle, even in winter." Eiders breeding in eastern Siberia, Alaska, and western Canada normally spend the winter months around the edges of the pack ice in the Bering Sea. Those from eastern Canada and western Greenland move to open water around southern Greenland, Labrador, and Newfoundland.

King eiders turn up with some regularity in winter along the New England coast, and references note that "small numbers penetrate the Great Lakes region" of the northern United States. Documented records do exist for winter strays in Florida, southern California, Kansas, and even Louisiana, so a king eider in Texas did not seem an impossibility. Clearly, however, it was improbable.

Then Jerry Caraviotis of the Houston Zoo reported to us that he and others had seen the stray eider on the beach not far from the Quintana jetty and obtained good photographs. The following morning, Tom Morris, cochair of the Migration Celebration, called to tell us the bird was again sitting on the beach, this time at a fishing pier near Quintana County Park. We arrived to find many other birders watching it with binoculars and spotting scopes. Many took pictures, and artists Mimi Hoppe Wolf and Maren Phillips, both present at the Celebration, made field sketches and watercolor paintings. There was no longer any question as to the bird's identity.

Immature king eider

Texas' king eider has now been seen by countless birders, and more continue to arrive from across the country. Reports have gone out on the Internet and on numerous Rare Bird Alerts.

In a severe state of molt, the bird probably cannot fly, and visitors to Quintana are urged to give it a wide berth and not approach too closely. Once its molt is complete, the king eider will probably head back northward to its customary Arctic waters, but for now, it is causing great excitement along our Texas coast.

It is impossible to say what brought the king eider to our shores, but whatever the motivation for its visit, it has become, by sheer necessity, a temporary Texas resident. Unlike most other birds that molt a few feathers at a time, waterfowl are "synchronous molters." That is, they change all of their old flight feathers over a brief period of two to four weeks, normally after the breeding season. During that time they are unable to fly, and they hide away in the marshes or take to the open sea. Because ducks have heavy bodies relative to the amount of wing surface, the loss of even a few wing feathers is a serious hindrance to their flying ability. Rather than molt a feather or two at a time, it is better for waterfowl to undergo a quick and total "overhaul."

Although the appearance of a king eider in the Gulf of Mexico is rare indeed, this is not an uncommon species in its normal environment. It can be very abundant along the coasts in the high Arctic regions of the world. Highly gregarious, king eiders migrate in long lines along the shores and over ice floes, landing to swim buoyantly in the storm-tossed seas. Flocks of as many as one hundred thousand molting eiders have been reported from Davis Strait off western Greenland, and estimates place the total king eider population of North America at one to one and one-half million birds.

The present Texas eider is without a doubt a young male, but opinions vary about its age. As previously noted, references differ as to whether king eiders reach adulthood in three or four years, and Frank Bellrose, in *Ducks, Geese and Swans of North America,* says that "males are in full adult plumage as they approach their second summer" and that a sizable proportion begin breeding at that age.

Bellrose further notes: "'Majestic' describes the male king eider, one of the larger ducks in North America." Other authors vote it one of the most beautiful of all waterfowl, and Kenn Kaufman, in *Lives of North American Birds,* calls it "strikingly ornate."

"Its regal head is characterized by a short orange bill sweeping upward into an orange knoblike frontal shield outlined in black and complemented by a pale blue crest," writes Bellrose. "The side of the male's head is pale green, and a black 'V' outlines the throat. The neck, chest, and foreback are cream-white. Black prevails over the lower back, rump, scapulars, tail coverts, breast, belly, and sides, but the tail is brown-black."

In contrast, the female lacks the large, distinctive frontal shield and is more drably attired in tawny brown, her feathers streaked and tipped with black. It is a plumage more suited to sitting quietly on her nest on the Arctic tundra, providing near-perfect camouflage against roving predators.

The king eider nests on small islands along the Arctic coasts or near inland tundra ponds, often selecting a barren slope overlooking the water. There the female makes a shallow depression and lines it with bits of plant material and large amounts of soft down from her breast. Her three to seven olive buff eggs hatch in twenty-three or twenty-four days, and she then leads her newly hatched ducklings to the water. Although the hen tends her young carefully, they quickly begin to find their own food. Bellrose further notes that "evidence indicates that young king eiders have an astonishingly rapid growth rate to reach flying stage in slightly over one month."

During the summer months, freshwater midge larvae and aquatic vegetation dominate the eider's diet. For most of the year, however, this sea duck subsists primarily on marine invertebrates acquired from the bottom. Indeed, king eiders have been recorded diving as deep as 180 feet in the frigid Bering Sea. Blue mussels and other mollusks make up as much as half of the seafood diet, while crabs, sand dollars, sea urchins, and sea anemones are taken in significant numbers. Smaller amounts of sea grasses and algae add variety.

The king eider is one of four eider species found around the world in Arctic seas. All are well protected from the chill waters by the dense "eiderdown" that has become famous as an insulating material in jackets and sleeping bags.

The scientific name of the genus, *Somateria*, reflects this attribute, for it comes from the Greek for "woolly bodied." The king eider is *Somateria spectabilis*, its specific epithet derived from the Latin for "conspicuous" or "remarkable." *Eider*, in turn, stems from the Old Norse and Icelandic names for these sea ducks.

The adult king eider truly is a spectacular bird, as its scientific name suggests. Hopefully, the young male currently staking its claim to a section of Texas beach near Quintana will survive to reach that plumage.

Sadly, this eider did not survive. Finally, as it became obviously weaker and weaker, it was taken into captivity for rehabilitation. It was found to be severely malnourished, perhaps because of a lack of appropriate food in the warm, shallow Gulf waters, and it soon died. In spite of its sad fate, however, this extraordinary bird was added to the official Texas list, and countless birders were able to see their first king eider, a rare bird indeed at this southern latitude.

No birder, no matter how experienced, can identify every bird seen in the field. Often the observation is too fleeting or made under poor light conditions. Heavy foliage may obscure key field marks, or the subject may simply be too far away for careful examination. Then, too, there are species so similar in appearance that they can be separated only by the most expert of observers, one who is intimately familiar with their plumages or perhaps recognizes their characteristic songs.

In the following column, written in 1976, none of these factors pertained, yet the subjects of the column were never identified. Highly qualified observers looked at them carefully, but twenty-seven years later, the birds remain unnamed. Some of those birders have forgotten the incident; others prefer not to discuss it, perhaps fearing scorn from the ornithological community.

Yet, in going back over our notes and the column written at the time, there is no question the birds existed. And there is little doubt in our minds that we had seen something highly unusual, probably a species unprecedented in the United States. There is no satisfying conclusion to the story; we still do not know what birds we encountered. They will forever remain a mystery, with no satisfying tick beside their name on our lists.

Two very mysterious birds have been causing a furor among local bird-watchers this spring. The reason for the excitement is that even though those birds have been carefully studied by highly experienced observers, the birds have not been positively identified. It appears likely that they belong to a species normally restricted to southern Mexico and Central America. It is also probable that the species has never before been seen in the United States.

The first reports were of a bird found by Jeffrey Glassberg *(now more familiar to nature enthusiasts as an author of butterfly guides and founder of the North American Butterfly Association)* and Hermann Bultmann of Rice University along the Dow Nature Trail near Lake Jackson in Brazoria County. They saw a flycatcher-like bird, somewhat larger than the orioles with which it was associating, and recognized it as something unusual. Glassberg and Bultmann reported the sighting to other birders, and soon a number of people from Houston, Freeport, and even Austin had arrived to see the strange visitor.

Between April 25 and May 2, 1976, the bird was seen repeatedly. It was generally described as being rusty brown on the head, back, and wings, with a somewhat lighter orange brown breast. Individual descriptions varied, perhaps because of different light conditions. Some thought the back appeared slightly olive brown; some thought the breast was more golden.

This variation in the descriptions is, in itself, worth noting. People see different things, depending on the light and their own perception of colors. Sunlight filtered through leaves gives a greenish cast, whereas early morning or late afternoon light is more golden. Brightly colored birds can even appear almost black from some angles. Thus, in field observations, it is always important to realize that the conditions can influence what you see, or think you see.

On most points, however, all observers agreed. There were no prominent markings of any kind, no wing bars or facial pattern. Some had at first thought it might be a female tanager, but this bird had the large-headed appearance and upright posture of a flycatcher. A careful search through various field guides led some to suspect that it might be a member of the cotinga family, a group of tropical American birds closely related to the flycatchers.

On one thing in particular their opinions were unanimous. This was not a bird with which the birders were familiar. It was obviously a bird that did not belong on the upper Texas coast.

Because of a number of other commitments, we did not get down to Lake Jackson to see that particular bird. On May 2, however, we were in Galveston County Park near League City to lead a field trip for the members of a bird-study class that John taught as part of the Contemporary Science Seminars program sponsored by the Houston Museum of Natural Science and the University of Houston.

Carl Aiken, assistant director of the museum and an experienced tropical birder, had come to help with the trip, and he was with a

Rufous mourner

portion of the group some distance away across the park. Walking over to us excitedly, he called our attention to a strange bird that he and some class members had observed. Perched high in the top of a dead tree was an orange brown bird with a golden orange breast. It had no other identifying features, but it sat upright as a flycatcher does and seemed to have a large, flycatcher head.

Although we saw this bird for only a short time, Aiken had studied it in detail for several minutes. All of us were convinced we had seen a bird closely matching the description of the Lake Jackson sighting. We were equally convinced it was a bird we had never seen before. A phone call later that day to Houston birder Margaret Anderson, who had been coordinating the information, revealed that the first bird had also been seen in Lake Jackson the same morning. Now there were two!

The following morning, we returned to the park, accompanied by Carl Aiken and equipped with cameras and long telephoto lenses. The trees that had been filled with migrating warblers the previous day were now empty. The birds had moved on. There would be no photographs of this mystery bird, and none was obtained of the one in Lake Jackson. It vanished the same day.

We have pored over bird books for hours, as have most of the others who saw either of the birds—books on Mexico, Central and

South America, the West Indies, Europe, and Asia. In the Mexican guides is a bird that resembles what we think we saw, one that fits most of the descriptions. It is a bird called the rufous mourner.

The mourner is, indeed, a rusty-colored bird about the size of our great crested flycatcher. The mourners are members of the tropical cotinga family but are closely related to the flycatchers. *(Most ornithologists have now placed the genus with the flycatchers.)*

But a rufous mourner in Texas is unprecedented. *Unthinkable* might be a better word. It is a bird found in lowland forests from southern Mexico to northwestern Ecuador. Displaced birds are usually those that migrate or wander long distances and become lost or caught up in storms. Admittedly, there were extremely high winds just prior to the sightings, winds strong enough to sink oil rigs in the Gulf of Mexico, but mourners do not migrate, and there is no reason they should venture out of the forest more than nine hundred miles away.

One consideration in reporting extreme rarities is that they may have escaped from captivity, but a check of Houston's Busch Bird Park and zoos in the surrounding area revealed no escaped birds fitting this description. These insect eaters are difficult to feed and seldom kept in captivity.

In an effort to resolve the problem, Dr. John O'Neill, renowned ornithologist, artist, and curator of the Museum of Vertebrate Zoology at Louisiana State University, brought specimens fitting the general description of the mystery birds to the Houston museum. With name tags hidden, they were examined by several people who had seen either one or both of the Texas birds. Each agreed, independently, that the two rufous mourner skins in O'Neill's collection best fit what he or she had seen. The others were all too small, too large, too dark, too light, or too streaked.

There the story ends. Were the birds we had seen the first North American mourners? Some think so, but no one knows for sure. Indeed, few would be willing to make the claim. One such bird would be highly unlikely; sighting two of them seems impossible. We agree that it is impossible, but we are still unable to find a more plausible solution. If we did not see a rufous mourner, we have absolutely no idea what we did see.

3

Games People Play

One of the busiest birding seasons of the year is the period that includes the Christmas holidays, for that is the time for the Audubon Society's Christmas Bird Count across the continent. Starting as a small, friendly competition in 1900, the count has grown through the years, with hundreds of participating areas and thousands of birders, and the tradition has spread from North America southward across the border to Latin America and the West Indies. Not only do these census efforts provide a year-to-year record of avian population trends but they offer fellowship and recreation for both experienced and novice birders alike.

Bird lovers join professional ornithologists in contributing to our knowledge of birds in other ways as well. Some band birds under permits from the U.S. Fish and Wildlife Service and state wildlife agencies. Others take part in citizen science projects such as feeder watches and breeding-bird surveys. There are now countless "big day" birding contests, in which teams see how many species they can record in a single day, and multiday competitions offer significant prize money to be contributed to conservation organizations.

A relatively recent development is the birding or nature festival, in which participants attend seminars, workshops, and field trips under the tutelage of expert speakers and guides. One of the first of these events in Texas was the Rockport-Fulton Hummer/Bird Celebration, and the phenomenal success of that event has spawned similar ones across the state. Currently, almost every region of the country has its *own birding festival, offering tremendous opportunities to see and learn about the birds and natural history of that area.*

A Holiday Happening: 1974

The following is an article that appeared in the Houston Chronicle *on December 21, 1974. It was, in a sense, an audition for the "Nature Trails" column that began several weeks later on February 15, 1975. Undoubtedly, the style of the writing changed through more than twenty-four years of writing the column, but we think this effort still conveys the essential elements of Christmas Bird Counts and the excitement of the chase. It appeared under the banner "Christmas Is for the Birds," a title chosen by one of the newspaper's editors.*

Christmas is a time of tradition: trees, lights, music, presents. But for some Houstonians, this is the season for another tradition—the seventy-fifth annual Christmas Bird Count.

Forsaking last-minute shopping, ovens full of cookies, and even television bowl games, the area's ardent bird-watchers are instead out wading marshes, prowling forests, and braving chill winds on deserted beaches. What prompts this mild but usually permanent form of insanity? A hunt for birds.

This is not a hunt with rifles or shotguns for a Christmas turkey or goose. Instead, the weapons are binoculars, spotting scopes, notebooks, and field guides. The purpose is a desire to contribute a small part to scientific knowledge and to share in friendly competition.

These one-day counts may be conducted any time between December 14 and December 31. (*The exact dates change each year and now extend over the New Year's weekend.*) This period covers three weekends and spreads out more than fifty different Texas counts, thereby allowing the most ardent birders (as they prefer to call themselves) to participate in several of them in the Houston area.

First on the schedule this year was the Bolivar Peninsula census on December 15. By foot and by car, birders scoured the area within a fifteen-mile circle to find about 145 different bird species. On December 22, almost a hundred people will converge on Freeport in an attempt to win back the mythical national championship by identifying more kinds of birds than any other count area does. And still later, on December 28, the Houston Christmas Count team takes the field. Centered in Baytown, but organized by the Ornithology Group of the Houston Outdoor Nature Club, this count is also expected to rank high in the national standings.

The whole thing started seventy-four years ago in 1900. Frank Chapman, editor of *Bird-Lore* magazine, proposed the Christmas Count as an alternative to "side hunts" in which hunting teams vied to see which side could kill the most game. Twenty-seven people in 25 locations across the country took part in that first count. Pacific Grove, California, emerged victorious with 36 species, and Chapman himself, in Englewood, New Jersey, finished second with 18.

The idea caught on, and under the sponsorship of the National Audubon Society and the U.S. Fish and Wildlife Service, the Christmas Count effort has grown each year. In 1973, a new high of 1,055 counts involved 24,863 participants. They counted a staggering total of more than 78 million individual birds.

The rules of the game are simple. Each census takes place within a carefully planned circle fifteen miles in diameter. These areas are usually chosen to provide as many different habitats—woods, marsh, fields, water—as possible, because each habitat has its own types of birds. Once established, the count circle is normally maintained throughout the years so that the continuing records indicate what is happening to bird populations. Occasionally, however, count areas must be changed as the traditional ones are inundated with subdivisions and industrial plants.

Each Christmas Bird Count is planned months in advance so that participants can be organized, become familiar with their areas, and above all, reserve that day for the birds. The circle is divided into smaller sections, each assigned to a team of birders who work together to count all the birds in that section.

Every robin and cardinal is added to the tally sheet, although not with as much delight as a rare peregrine falcon or yellow rail. A notation of 30,000 red-winged blackbirds flying overhead is obviously an estimate but probably not far from the actual number. Much of the scientific value of the Christmas Count lies in these numbers of each species, which can be compared from year to year. The friendly competition, however, comes from trying to spot the greatest number of species.

An official count lasts twenty-four hours—from midnight to midnight. Most of the birders hit the ground running at dawn and do not give up until it is too dark to tell a woodpecker from a hummingbird. The hardiest souls may spend several hours in the dark trying to find one of the five kinds of local owls needed for a successful count.

Cars, boats, and swamp buggies are all used for transportation. This year the Freeport group plans to use a small airplane in an effort to spot an elusive bald eagle. But mostly the birders walk, and wade, and fight mud and briars and mosquitoes. As dusk nears, they search frantically for species they have missed.

Tired, dirty, and hungry, the counters meet at a previously appointed restaurant or home for the postmortem. This is birding's social event of the year. Old friends greet each other across the room,

Peregrine falcon

Our Life with Birds

often too hungry and tired to get up from their food. Teams compile their area checklists, and the count coordinator then reads the master list as the excitement grows. Sightings of rare birds are exclaimed over, and absent species elicit loud groans. When a committee of experts has ruled on questionable sightings, the number of species is announced. Loud cheers greet a successful effort, and talk turns to whether the total will be high enough to beat Cocoa, Florida, or perhaps San Diego, California. Then planning begins for next year's count.

The more than 1,000 Christmas Counts are conducted in every U.S. state and Canadian province. Last year, Mexico and the West Indies also contributed. These new tropical counts promise tremendous new totals and fascinating birds to those who can participate in them. Christmas Counts also are catching on in other countries, although the results are not compiled with the ones from North America.

Because many birds tend to move south in winter, the milder climates produce the highest counts. Coastal birders also have the advantage of finding both land and water species. For these reasons, Texas, California, and Florida produce the largest lists in the United States each year. The upper Texas coast provides a nearly ideal location for Christmas birding, for resident species in a wide variety of habitats are joined by strays from West and South Texas as well as northern birds driven southward by ice and snow.

In fact, Freeport holds the North American record *(since broken by other Texas counts)* with 226 different species of birds recorded in 1971. In 1972, Freeport repeated as champion, sharing a total of 209 with Cocoa, Florida. Last year, Cocoa managed a count of 210, with Freeport and San Diego tied for second at 201. On Sunday, the Freeport team, organized by the Houston Audubon Society under the leadership of Houstonian Victor Emanuel *(now renowned as the founder of Victor Emanuel Nature Tours)*, hopes to regain the title.

Providing stark contrast to these prestigious counts are those conducted by dedicated and hardy birders in more northern climates. Last year three observers in Bancroft, Ontario, spent nine hours in the field in a foot of snow and seventeen-below-zero temperatures. They recorded a total of 45 individual birds of only 5 species. Two birders in Whitehorse, Yukon Territory (twenty below zero), fared slightly better with 7 species and 221 individuals. Klukwan, Alaska, checked in with 16 species and 878 birds, but a fantastic 634 of those were bald eagles.

Once the fun of the Christmas Counts is over, the scientific evaluation begins. This is the real worth of the massive project. Data from all of the counts are compiled, computerized, and reported in the Audubon Society's *American Birds*. From these statistics professional and amateur ornithologists study species distribution and population changes. The decline of the brown pelican on the Texas coast can be followed in count records, as can that of many other vanishing birds. Other species may be increasing or expanding their range into new areas. Bird-density maps from the counts will even be studied by the air force in an effort to schedule training flights in areas free of large flocks of birds.

As Texas Christmas Counts continue through the holidays, it is doubtful that any of the birders will be faced with the twenty-below-zero temperatures of the Yukon. But if they should, it is a safe bet they would still be out. One recent Houston count was marked by hordes of mosquitoes in ninety-degree weather. The next year, it was thirty-four degrees and raining.

When questioned about his bandaged hands at the Freeport postcount dinner last year, a young birder reported nonchalantly that he had been washed off the end of the jetty by heavy seas. He was now comfortably dry in borrowed clothes but still grieving the loss of a valuable spotting scope. *(This young birder was Kenn Kaufman, now one of the best-known bird experts and authors in the country. His Christmas Count experience was included in his book* Kingbird Highway, *detailing his record-setting year in pursuit of birds.)*

What kinds of people have this seemingly incurable disease? Young, old, men, women, doctors, lawyers, teachers, students, postal workers, salespeople. They have in common a great love of the outdoors and a particular love of birds. The Houston team had 63 participants in 1973, and Freeport had 78. Oakland, California, put an amazing 260 birders on its roster.

And what do they get for their efforts? Exercise, enjoyment, competition, a hearty appetite, and a feeling that they have helped contribute to our growing knowledge of birds.

If you think this sounds like fun, put a bird count on your Christmas list. Even beginners are valuable in keeping records, and a day in the field with experts is a great way to learn. You might even be the one to spot that bald eagle. And who knows, this might even be the year for a partridge in a pear tree!

The Changing Scene: 1990

The 1989–90 season's Freeport Christmas Bird Count tied its own all-time North American record of 226 species set in 1971, and it is interesting to compare those two record counts held nearly two decades apart. They mirror a number of changes that have taken place through the years, not only in bird populations but in our knowledge of the birds and their habits.

The first difference is strictly one of nomenclature. The lovely and graceful white-tailed kite is now called the black-shouldered kite. *(However, that taxonomy has now been reversed by the American Ornithologists' Union, and the name has more recently reverted to white-tailed kite.)* The long-billed and short-billed marsh wrens are simply the marsh wren and the sedge wren, respectively. There are no longer marsh hawks and sparrow hawks; they have been replaced by northern harriers and American kestrels. The changes are part of an effort to adopt a more cosmopolitan system of names in agreement with those used in Europe and around the world.

Included in the total of 1971 were the blue goose and Harlan's hawk, birds not found on the 1989 list. They are now considered merely forms of the snow goose and red-tailed hawk and are no longer counted separately in official totals.

The earlier list contains pairs of both Baltimore and Bullock's orioles, birds that are now known to be the eastern and western races of a single species, the northern oriole. *(That decision has also been reversed, reinstating Baltimore and Bullock's orioles to full species status.)*

Likewise, the stray Audubon's warbler among nine hundred myrtle warblers in 1971 would merely have been regarded as the western subspecies of what is now collectively called the yellow-rumped warbler in the latest Christmas Count.

Now, however, birders record both great-tailed and boat-tailed grackles, two distinct species that were formerly considered one. They are distinguished by eye color and voice and do not seem to interbreed where their ranges meet on the upper Texas coast. This has resulted in the gain of a species in the win-a-few, lose-a-few battle birders wage with taxonomy.

Earlier Christmas Counts always listed large numbers of semipalmated sandpipers wintering along the Texas coast. They are difficult to distinguish from western sandpipers in nonbreeding plumage, and field guides formerly mentioned the longer bill of the western as a diagnostic mark. Recently, however, ornithologists have discovered that bill lengths overlap, and that previous wintering semipalms were misidentified. That species is now known to spend Christmas far south of our borders, and few modern-day birders have the temerity to claim a winter sighting. There were seventeen in 1971, but none in 1989.

The rock dove, or feral pigeon, was not counted in 1971. Because it is obviously reproducing freely on its own outside captivity, it is now included on the official list. (*The name has even more recently been changed by the AOU to rock pigeon.*)

A more welcome addition to recent Texas counts is the brown pelican. Thankfully, this characteristic coastal bird is recovering from the brink of extinction, and 217 were seen in Freeport this season where there were none in 1971.

Aided by better guidebooks and optical gear, birders have learned a great deal more about their quarry's habits, and their identification skills have improved accordingly. Spotters now take up cold, wet stations on the Freeport area's Surfside and Quintana jetties to count gannets, jaegers, scoters, and other seabirds that were rarely seen in the 1970s. Few birders even knew they entered Texas waters.

Similarly, a "hummingbird patrol" has encouraged neighborhood feeders and found an amazing number of these tiniest of birds. The

Semipalmated sandpiper

1971 record list contained three hummingbirds, each of a different species. The 1989 effort found twenty-three birds of seven species, and yet another kind showed up the following day.

Thus, there have been many changes through the years, even though the totals are the same. Best of all, perhaps, is that 159 people turned out for the latest count, compared with 87 in 1971. More than 40,000 birders now participate in more than fifteen hundred Christmas Counts, and that is good for both the birders and the birds.

Crazy Counters: 1995

Anticipation runs high as we leave home at 5:00 A.M. even though a light rain is falling. Radio reports threaten severe thunderstorms throughout the day, but we continue on toward the bursts of lightning that streak an ominous southern sky. This, after all, is December 17, the day of the Freeport Christmas Bird Count. Through our thirty years of participation in the yearly census, we have missed only a few for family emergencies. Rain or shine, heat or cold, the count goes on.

The Freeport count was founded in 1957 by sixteen-year-old Victor Emanuel, now a well-known nature-tour leader. With five observers, he recorded 105 species. By 1970, its ranks swelling to fifty-five birders, Freeport totaled 204 species, second highest in the country.

Since that time, Freeport has finished first sixteen times and never ranked lower than a tie for second until last year, when its total was exceeded by Corpus Christi and a new Texas count at Mad Island Marsh. Only in 1976, in the face of persistent rain, did the day's total of 196 fall below the magic 200 mark.

By the time we reach our portion of the count circle at Surfside, however, we know we face mounting odds. Severe-weather alerts blanket the region, and gusty winds rock our van. Our efforts will be further hampered by the government shutdown that prohibits access to Brazoria National Wildlife Refuge, a cornerstone of the Freeport count.

As we wait for dawn, a short-eared owl sails past from deep in the marsh. The first bird of the day, and one that can be difficult to find, it offers a ray of hope amid gloomy predictions. A flaming sun rises through a narrow slit above the pounding surf and disappears immediately into turbulent black clouds. Darkness envelops us again, and jagged lightning forks down all around.

We head for a patch of woodland beside a bayou, hoping to search the thickets before the rain begins in earnest. Wading through waist-high briars, we locate cedar waxwings and a palm warbler among the more common American goldfinches and swamp sparrows. A gray catbird answers our whistled calls, and a song sparrow pops up in the underbrush to investigate the sound.

The cheerful notes of Carolina chickadees herald a mixed feeding flock of small birds, and we pick out the usual tufted titmice, yellow-rumped and orange-crowned warblers, ruby-crowned kinglets, and a house wren. They move into a cluster of live oaks, and we can barely see them in the fading light. We detect a blue-gray gnatcatcher by its whining call, but a mysterious warbler escapes without a name.

Short-eared owl

The promised deluge makes further pursuit impractical, and we drive instead to a levee overlooking the tidal marsh. Setting up a spotting scope in the lee of our vehicle, we sort out five yellow-crowned night-herons among their abundant black-crowned cousins. There are roseate spoonbills and black-necked stilts, both species that move southward in winter and can be hard to locate on demand.

At noon, we meet area leader David Veselka and his party to review our progress; however, it proves difficult to plot strategy in a driving rain. In desperation, we separate again to search any location we can reach.

Through the afternoon we pick up a pair of common goldeneyes near the jetty and red-breasted mergansers in the Intracoastal Canal. We have a wonderful close-up encounter with an American bittern, one of our favorite birds, and we locate a marbled godwit wading with long-billed curlews on the edge of the marsh. Ospreys, American avocets, and a gull-billed tern are added to our list.

Among the beach homes in Surfside we discover three bronzed

cowbirds with a flock of red-winged blackbirds. This is a South Texas specialty often missed on the Freeport count and gives us a brief ray of mental sunshine.

The highlight of our day, however, proves to be a young male yellow-headed blackbird in an enormous mixed flock of blackbirds and grackles. Discovered independently by Veselka's group, it will later be voted "best bird" of this year's count, having been seen only once in previous years.

Dusk comes early beneath turbulent skies, and we assemble as usual at the Dow company cafeteria for a welcome supper and countdown meeting. Most of the participants have been soaked to the skin, and we hear reports that the area had six to ten inches of rain through the day. Most sobering, certainly, is the sighting of a waterspout that hurled a floating timber across the jetty on which some adventuresome birders were stationed.

As Emanuel compiles the list, it becomes quickly obvious that we will not break 200 species again this year. No one reports an American oystercatcher or a groove-billed ani; there are no black-and-white warblers or red-headed woodpeckers. Without the Brazoria refuge, we failed to locate elusive king and yellow rails and a Henslow's sparrow.

When he calls out "bald eagle" and there is only silence, Emanuel notes wryly that it was "a bad day for eagles." More embarrassing is the lack of least sandpipers, and we wish we had spent more time wading the grassy edges of the marsh to find their refuge from the storm.

Few rare "bonus birds" are added to the normal list. Joining the yellow-headed blackbird are Franklin's gull, red knot, pomarine jaeger, buff-bellied hummingbird, house finch, and an unidentified swallow. The total stands at 188 species, lowest in three decades, but a creditable list in the worst weather on record.

Perhaps the best comment of the day comes from the owner of a local convenience store where Emanuel and his party stop for a quick lunch. "You guys are crazy," she says on learning they are going back out into the field. Few among the eighty hard-core participants would argue the point, but most will return again next year, come rain or shine.

Gatherings of Birders: 1995

A new trend in birding is sweeping the country. Annual bird festivals are springing up in cities and towns from Florida to Alaska and from the wave-washed New England coast to the arid deserts of the Southwest. An obvious step in the rapid rise of ecotourism, most festivals combine the efforts of birders and nature groups with those of local chambers of commerce, often with participation by state and federal agencies. They benefit both the communities involved and broader conservation efforts.

National groups such as the Audubon Society and the American Birding Association, of course, have held conferences for many years, as have state ornithological societies and research groups. Although they attract many new birders, these meetings have focused largely on those already dedicated to the sport, "preaching to the choir" as the saying goes.

The newer festivals cater to the beginner as well as the ardent birder, seeking to awaken an interest in the novice and to appeal to the entire family. For a few days, or over a single weekend, they offer guided field trips, stimulating speakers, and booths displaying nature-related items and supplies. The events are crash courses in birding and nature observation, while at the same time offer a chance to meet others with similar interests.

Programs often revolve around a specific bird of the locality. Hummingbirds, bluebirds, whooping and sandhill cranes, and bald eagles are all honored by one or more celebrations. There are numerous shorebird festivals and even a pelican festival. Other events feature the unique bird-watching opportunities of particular regions: the tropical birds of the Rio Grande Valley or the specialties of southeastern Arizona.

Although birds hold center stage, other aspects of nature also receive attention. Many festivals have speakers who discuss landscaping to attract wildlife, conservation issues, wildlife photography, and even bats and reptiles. In the coming months, we will be speaking at Texas birding festivals not only on bird banding and migration but on butterflies and backyard nature. Most programs offer something for every taste.

Texas ranks near the forefront of this relatively new development in ecotourism. At least nine different events are slated across the state during the remainder of the year, including several making their debut.

Rockport-Fulton's famed Hummer/Bird Celebration was the first of its kind in our state and developed around the enormous number of ruby-throated hummingbirds that congregate along that portion of the coast during their fall migration. Townspeople put up feeders and open their yards to attendees of the Celebration, and it is not unusual to see a hundred or more of the tiny, gemlike hummingbirds swirling around a single flower bed or its complementary bank of sugar-water tubes. Most are eastern ruby-throats, but black-chinned, rufous, and buff-bellied hummingbirds also show up.

The seventh annual Hummer/Bird Celebration takes place September 7–10 this year, with almost continuous programs through the four-day event. Speakers include prolific authors Paul Johnsgard, Pete Dunne, Sally and Andy Wasowski, and fourteen others, most of them repeating their talks at two different times to facilitate scheduling. There will also be numerous bus and boat trips to view local birds.

Famed field-guide author, painter, and photographer Roger Tory Peterson will also be present to help dedicate the Great Texas Coastal Birding Trail and the Connie Hagar Cottage Sanctuary (*sadly, Roger passed away shortly after this event*). A pioneering Texas birder, Hagar put Rockport on the ornithological map, and the birding trail is a major development in ecotourism that is being imitated in many other states.

A new feature of the Hummer/Bird Celebration this year is a special youth program with two days of workshops and bird walks catering to the interests of schoolchildren. Some of the same expert speakers will help them learn about the treats that nature offers everyone.

Rockport-Fulton's effort has grown enormously through the years. Three thousand people participated last year, and there was national publicity in magazines and newspapers and on network television.

On November 8–12, the birding world will journey to Harlingen, Texas, for the second annual Rio Grande Valley Birding Festival. Keynote speakers include Kenn Kaufman, Chandler Robbins, Bill Clark, and June Osborne, each a published author of bird books and field guides. Daytime programs range from "Birding 101" to "The Wildlife Garden."

In its first year, the Harlingen event attracted one thousand people and brought an estimated $266,000 to the region. This year's festival is expected to draw eighteen hundred birders and an extra $1.3 million in revenue. Clearly, birding festivals have become big business for chambers of commerce and local merchants, but they also aid the featured birds. Conservation and business groups work hand in hand, a welcome partnership that has been long in coming. Increased awareness of wildlife values and habitat preservation benefits both the human and avian populations.

The Harlingen festival owes a portion of its success to its location near the Rio Grande. Birders come from across the continent to spot chachalacas, green jays, great kiskadees, Altamira orioles, and other species that range no farther north. Daily guided field trips at extremely modest prices offer the best birding the country has to offer.

Other communities are also capitalizing on their unique resources. In the spring, the Brazosport area will hold its second annual Migration Celebration; Eagle Lake, its second Attwater's Prairie-Chicken Festival. In May, the Texas State Railroad and Partners in Flight will hold a Birding by Rail Getaway Weekend centered in

Great kiskadee

Palestine, Texas. *(Several other Texas birding festivals have been organized since this column was written, and the trend continues.)*

Birding festivals offer a unique and enjoyable opportunity to learn about nature from qualified speakers and tour leaders in the company of others with similar interests. There is no better way to expand your outdoor horizons. We suggest you try one; you will like it.

Birds with Bracelets: 1976

For everyone interested in birds, professional and amateur ornithologists alike, there is a lot of truth in that old adage "A bird in the hand is worth two in the bush." By putting a numbered aluminum band on the leg of that bird, it is possible to learn a great deal about its habits and travels.

The idea of being able to mark and recognize individual birds has intrigued scientists for hundreds of years. The first known banding experiments were performed in Germany in 1740, when strings were tied around the legs of young swallows in an attempt to learn about their migrations. In 1803, Audubon banded young phoebes with silver threads and found that two of them returned the following summer.

Bird banding was organized under federal supervision in 1920, and today there are more than two thousand banders in the United States and Canada. Other countries around the world also have active banding projects, although many of the latter call the process "ringing."

Several million birds have received the shiny little bracelets, and the massive data files on all these birds are maintained by the U.S. Fish and Wildlife Service at its Bird Banding Laboratory in Laurel, Maryland. Most of the people who subscribe to this effort are amateurs, people like us who enjoy birds and wish to contribute to our understanding of them. It is a challenging and rewarding hobby.

There is an indescribable thrill in being able to hold this fragile beauty in the hand, to feel both the delicacy and the strength of an organism weighing only a few ounces and yet capable of nonstop

Eastern phoebe

flight across an ocean. This is a chance to admire the myriad colors that make birds some of the world's most beautiful creatures and then to release that beauty unharmed.

Because banding is a complex process, however, and because of the large amount of bookkeeping required to coordinate the field-work, a special license is required. In fact, the bander in Texas must hold both federal and state permits before he or she can legally capture a bird. The bands are distributed only to those who are working on scientific projects approved by the Banding Laboratory.

There are many different methods for capturing the birds to be banded. Young birds may receive their bands before they leave the nest, enabling ornithologists to study a known group of siblings. Many types of traps are also used to catch adult birds, including the large cannon nets employed by many game agencies for capturing waterfowl.

The most popular method for songbirds, however, is the use of nets made of very fine nylon or polyester mesh known as "mist nets." Most are made in Japan and can be purchased only by someone with a valid federal license. Thirty or more feet long and about eight feet high, they are stretched between poles across flyways or near feeding and watering areas. Any bird that chances to fly into this nearly invisible web is entangled and held securely without injury.

A feeling of excitement always accompanies a check of the waiting mist net. The bander may be faced with the task of releasing a fierce, defiant hawk or a tiny, fragile hummingbird. John was once stabbed in the face by a kingfisher's bill when he got careless, and we have both been bitten on the fingers until they bled by pugnacious cardinals and grosbeaks.

Each bird gets a uniquely numbered band of the proper size, bands that are issued in series by the Laboratory and must be individually reported. In addition to recording the band number and species of the bird and the date and location in which it was captured, the bander may record other data as well. Each bird is weighed and measured, and notes are taken on its age, sex, breeding status, and the condition of the plumage. Signs of illness, injury, or parasites are noted, and in some projects blood samples are taken for the study of communicable diseases. All data are taken quickly and the bird released to continue on its way, hopefully to be caught again someday.

If another bander captures a bird that has already been banded, that number is reported to the Banding Laboratory. Anyone finding a banded bird is also asked to send the band to the Fish and Wildlife Service in Washington, D.C. The finder receives a certificate stating when and where the bird was banded; the original bander is notified of the recovery, and another bit of data is added to our knowledge of birds.

What is the value of bird banding? What kind of information can be gained by trapping birds and placing numbered aluminum rings on their legs? From banding data come answers to such questions as "How long do wild birds live?" For only by being able to identify individuals can we determine their life spans.

Maximum known ages for most species range from ten to fifteen years, with a few, generally the larger birds, surviving for twenty or even thirty years. These are the exceptions, the avian equivalents of humans who make news by living beyond the century mark. Few wild birds survive their first year.

We can also find out where birds go in migration and how fast they fly. One banded ruddy turnstone, for example, was recovered twenty-five hours later and some five hundred miles away. An Arctic tern, a champion long-distance flier, was subsequently retrapped almost nine thousand miles from its initial capture site.

The number of banded birds recovered is extremely small. Most are never caught again, nor are they found dead. The vast majority become food for other creatures, vanish in hazardous ocean storms, or perish unseen in forests and fields. Yet, through the cooperation of thousands of people, our knowledge slowly grows. Each new bit of data—each bird marked years ago or miles away—is an exciting event for the bander.

Much remains to be learned about our common resident birds as well. For example, do you have a cardinal that frequents your backyard? Is he, or she, always there to whistle a cheerful greeting from the back fence or eat sunflower seeds at your feeder? Perhaps. But perhaps not.

We thought we had such faithful cardinals until we provided them with bands so that we could tell one from another. So far, there have been forty-five different birds in one year. Some are more faithful than others and have been caught several times at different seasons. They obviously remain in the neighborhood. Others have been banded and never seen again, their places taken by newcomers to our yard. It is difficult to recognize the players without a scorecard.

Blue jays, too, come and go. They are apparently even more migratory and prone to wander than are cardinals, and we were surprised to catch sixty-five different ones in our small backyard. Several stayed year-round, but others wandered through only during the last week of April and the first two weeks of May.

More reliable are the two Carolina wrens that received their bracelets the first time they flew into our nets in 1974. They are wiser now and avoid being caught, but we often see them patrolling the patio for insects and spiders. They have raised at least two broods of young (which we have also banded) in the yard and evidently protect their territory jealously, for we have never seen an unbanded wren in the area.

One day last winter we were pleased to see five purple finches at our feeders. These handsome little birds breed along the northern border of the country and in the coniferous forests of Canada. Only in the cold of winter do some of them wander south to visit the Houston area.

We quickly set up our nets in hopes of banding these finches, and you can imagine our surprise when we had captured 50 after the first three days. During the month they remained in our yard, we banded a total of 111 purple finches, yet seldom saw more than 5 or 6 at one time. Only by tagging individual birds could we accurately estimate the population.

Interesting, too, was an analysis of the age and sex of these fugitives from snow and ice. Male purple finches sport lovely reddish purple plumage from which the species gets its name. They do not get this plumage, however, until their second year, and young birds less than fifteen or sixteen months old are brown and heavily streaked like the mature females. Of the 111 finches captured, only 6 were purple adult males. Assuming an equal number of adult females (and we have no reason to believe the sexes should differ substantially in number), this means that more than 90 percent of the birds were immatures hatched that year. Few wild birds survive to a ripe old age, even by avian standards.

These are only a few examples of the information that can be gained by banding birds. Those purple finches first showed up in our yard a year ago this weekend, and we are eagerly watching the feeders in hopes they will come again this year to add their numbers to the record book.

Immature purple finch

Our Life with Birds

The Gold Rush of Winter: 1996

Few birds bring us more enjoyment at this season of the year than the American goldfinches that inhabit our own backyard. Highly social during the winter months, goldfinches travel in flocks that swirl through the treetops and forage in the shrubbery and across the lawn. They appear just after sunrise every day and remain until late afternoon, filling the perches of every feeder to dine on the sunflower and niger seeds that fuel their tiny bodies against the long, chilly nights.

Although members of the flock occasionally jockey for position in a flurry of wings, there are few major squabbles. Goldfinches seem to be amiable birds. Their constant activity and cheerful, twittering calls of *per-chick-o-ree,* or *just-look-at-me,* make them one of the most popular of all bird species at Houston-area feeders.

Its selection as the official state bird of three different states illustrates the widespread popularity of the American goldfinch. New Jersey on the eastern seaboard, Washington in the Pacific Northwest, and Iowa in the nation's heartland have all honored this pretty finch. It breeds across southern Canada and in all but the most southerly portions of the United States and spends the winter months from the northern tier of states to Mexico. Although a common winter resident throughout most of Texas, the goldfinch remains to breed only sparingly in the far northeastern corner of the state.

In breeding plumage, the male is a bright, glowing golden yellow with a small black cap and black wings and tail. White wing bars and white feather edgings on the tail contrast sharply with the black background. He is the only small yellow bird with black wings and is sometimes dubbed the "wild canary."

The female wears less striking garb. Olive green above and paler yellow below, she lacks the black cap and the bright yellow shoulder patches on her brownish black wings.

The winter plumage we usually see in Texas, however, is much less colorful. Most goldfinches are now greenish or grayish brown above and pale gray below, with only traces of the characteristic golden hue. Males usually display more yellow than their consorts, with scattered black feathers on their heads and contrasting black-and-white wings.

Arriving in our area in autumn, goldfinches sometimes linger until late spring, for they move northward to nest later in the season than most other birds. Only when the thistles and other wild-flowers go to seed do they pair off and begin their household chores, thereby assuring a plentiful supply of food for their growing young.

Goldfinches normally change mates between breeding seasons, and it is the female that shows nest-site fidelity, often returning to her old territory year after year. She places her compact, cuplike nest in the fork of a shrub or tree, usually near a pond or stream. Carefully woven of plant fibers and lined with thistledown, it is so tightly constructed that it may fill with water during a heavy rain unless sheltered by the incubating or brooding parent.

The female builds the nest and incubates her four to six pale bluish white eggs alone, but her attentive mate collects nesting material for her and feeds her as she sits. Both then feed the young on a mash of regurgitated thistle and other seeds, an unusual diet for baby birds. Adults, too, are primarily seedeaters, consuming only occasional insects and berries. Hence their penchant for feeders and their popularity as backyard birds.

Although common throughout East Texas from November into April, American goldfinches normally descend on our feeders about Christmastime and remain only until late February or early March. They seem to prefer natural foods when those are available, and they are particularly fond of the seeds of the cedar elms that grow throughout our neighborhood.

Possessing the required federal and state banding permits, we capture our goldfinches in traps and place the numbered aluminum bands around their legs. Released unharmed, these uniquely marked birds then provide us with information about their lives and movements through the seasons.

As we write this column in mid-January, we have already banded 250 finches, and there will be many more through the next two months. (We would eventually band more than 1,500 that season in *our small suburban back-yard.)* Last year we caught 660 of the little five-inch birds, and we hope to welcome many of them back again this year.

At any given time, we may have 50 or more finches swirling around the yard, and one might suspect that the same birds remain throughout the daylight hours and return again the following day. Such is not the case. Even after we had banded 600 birds, fewer than one-

American goldfinch

fourth of those we captured were wearing our bands. This indicates there must be an enormous pool of more than 2,000 goldfinches that circulates throughout the area; only a small portion use our feeders on any given day.

Twenty-eight finches caught last year had been banded in previous years; three of them returned three years in a row. So far, we have recovered one from the 1995 group and one that was banded in our yard in 1993. It returned unerringly to the same feeders after three trips to and from its distant breeding grounds.

One of our banded goldfinches was caught six years later in Alabama; another, four years later in Louisiana. Conversely, we trapped birds banded the previous year in Wisconsin and Michigan. Our favorite, however, is one of last winter's birds that turned up a few months later in Little Falls, Minnesota, very near our own childhood homes.

Although goldfinches appear to be plump little birds, they are surprisingly small beneath their fluffy plumage. Each weighs less than half an ounce, and two of them could be mailed back north with a single postage stamp.

Games People Play   77

Our detailed weight studies reveal that the finches lose an average of 15 percent of their weight overnight and gain it back by gorging on seeds throughout the day. One bird caught at 5:00 P.M. and again at 8:00 the next morning had lost 22 percent of its body weight. Obviously, the margin of safety is small, and birds that do not find food quickly after a cold night may perish within hours. The day-to-day life of an American goldfinch is tenuous at best.

We look forward to the arrival of the goldfinches every winter and regret seeing them go again in spring. During their visit, however, they fill our yard with charm and cheerfulness.

4

Variations on a Theme

Although all birds share certain characteristics that place them in the scientific class Aves, there are innumerable variations on the theme. Someone introduced to birds for the very first time, for example, would scarcely believe that a tiny hummingbird that swirls ceaselessly around a flower on flickering wings is even remotely related to the enormous, and flightless, ostrich, the largest of our present-day birds. Both, however, are covered with feathers of one form or another, and both reproduce by laying eggs.

Within the anatomical framework of the class, each species possesses unique modifications for the particular life it leads. There are different kinds of feathers for different purposes, and birds' beaks, feet, and eyes also reflect myriad adaptations for finding food and for surviving. Some birds wear colorful plumage to advertise their presence to competitors or potential mates; others have remarkable camouflage patterns for a more secretive lifestyle. These differences combine to make the study of birds a fascinating pursuit.

Adventurers and Their Namesakes: 1997

Anatomical characteristics are often reflected in the names we apply to birds, as are variations in song, the geographic range of the species, and particular habits or habitats. Many birds, too, are namesakes of early naturalists, and the origins of those names reveal much about the ornithological history of our country.

Watching Ken Burns's excellent PBS television series on the travels of Meriwether Lewis and William Clark, we were more impressed than ever with the incredible feat of these great explorers. In their 1804 expedition up the Missouri River and across the uncharted Rocky Mountains to the Pacific Coast, the Corps of Discovery opened the West to early scientists as well as to future pioneers and settlers.

In spite of the rigors of their journey, Captains Lewis and Clark managed to collect a host of previously unknown plants and animals. In so doing, they guaranteed for themselves a prominent place in the history of our country and in the annals of natural science. Ornithologically, the name of Meriwether Lewis lives on in Lewis' woodpecker, a large and unusual woodpecker of the western states with a greenish black head and back, dark red face, and pinkish belly. Clark's avian namesake is the Clark's nutcracker, a relative of the jays and crows. This large bird, known locally as the "camp robber" for its gregarious and aggressive antics around picnic areas and campgrounds, is common in the coniferous forests of the West.

One of the most familiar names in early American ornithology, of course, is that of John James Audubon. Audubon's shearwater, Audubon's oriole, and Audubon's warbler all bear his name, although the warbler has more recently been combined with its eastern counterpart, the myrtle warbler, under the less evocative name of yellow-rumped warbler.

An immigrant to the United States from Scotland in 1766, Alexander Wilson was educated in neither science nor art. In 1802, however, he conceived the idea of producing a series of illustrated volumes on the ornithology of the eastern states. The first was published in 1808, and by the time of Wilson's death in 1813, the eighth volume was at the printer. Wilson's work served as a model for many who followed in his footsteps, and he was honored with Wilson's storm-petrel, Wilson's plover, Wilson's phalarope, and Wilson's warbler.

Our Life with Birds

Born in England in 1789, William Swainson collected scientific specimens in many parts of the world and published prolifically. Among the greatest of his works was *Fauna Boreali-Americana,* a classic on the northern regions of the New World. Swainson scored what might be considered an ornithological hat trick; a hawk, a warbler, and a thrush now bear his name.

John Cassin (1813–69) was a Pennsylvania Quaker who became one of the best of a group of naturalists headquartered at the Philadelphia Academy of Natural Sciences. Although primarily a businessman, he found the time and energy to catalog the bird collection at the Academy, and he was described by fellow ornithologist Elliott Coues as the only person who was as familiar with the avifauna of the Old World as with that of America. Cassin accompanied Admiral Perry on his historic voyage to Japan and was published widely in the ornithological literature. Today his name lives on not only in his own publications but in the Cassin's auklet, kingbird, sparrow, and finch.

Many assume that Lincoln's sparrow is the namesake of the great U.S. president, but such is not the case. The name actually honors Thomas Lincoln of Maine. At the age of twenty-one, Lincoln sailed with Audubon on an 1833 trip along the Canadian coast. Near the mouth of the Natashquan River in Quebec, Audubon heard a sweet, liquid birdsong he did not recognize. Lincoln slipped through the woods and succeeded in finding the bird. It proved to be a new species, the only one collected on the expedition, and Audubon named it in the young man's honor.

Much more famous in scientific circles was Spencer Fullerton Baird. Born in Pennsylvania in 1823, Baird played an enormous role in the development of natural-history studies in the West and eventually rose to become secretary of the Smithsonian Institution. In regular contact with Audubon and countless other expedition leaders, he was the first to describe numerous species they collected. His associates, in turn, applied his name to Baird's sandpiper and Baird's sparrow.

The list goes on and on, through scores of avian species. There are such seabirds as Buller's shearwater, Leach's storm-petrel, and Brandt's cormorant. Heermann's, Franklin's, Bonaparte's, and

Lincoln's sparrow

Thayer's gulls inhabit North America's shores, as do the little Kittlitz's, Xantus', and Craveri's murrelets. Birders seek Bendire's and Le Conte's thrashers; Nuttall's and Strickland's woodpeckers *(the U.S. species of the latter is now called the Arizona woodpecker);* and Townsend's, Kirtland's, and MacGillivray's warblers.

The discoverer of the elegant Ross' gull that inhabits the high Arctic was James Clark Ross (1800–62), who collected the first specimen on the northern end of Hudson Bay in 1823. Ross went to sea when he was only twelve years old and spent much of his life exploring the Arctic regions. With Ross on an expedition to search for the Northwest Passage was Edward Sabine, for whom Sabine's gull was named.

One might expect that Ross' goose was also named for this explorer, but John Cassin named the little white goose for Bernard Rogan Ross (1827–74), an officer in the Hudson's Bay Company, who collected numerous specimens to send to Spencer Baird at the Smithsonian.

Steller's jay, Steller's eider, and Steller's sea-eagle were named for German naturalist Georg Wilhelm Steller, who accompanied the Russian expedition led by Vitus Bering to explore Alaska.

Scott's oriole may be the only bird named by one army general for another. Darius Nash Couch took a leave of absence from the army in 1853–54 to collect specimens in Mexico, and he named one of the new species he found after General Winfield Scott, with whom Couch had served. There is no evidence that Scott was interested in natural history, but Couch contributed enormously to our biological knowledge of the Southwest. His name is still used for Couch's kingbird as well as Couch's spadefoot toad.

Much of our nation's early history is bound up in the names of birds. Behind each species—Forster's tern, Harris' hawk, Bewick's wren, Le Conte's sparrow, and many more–lies an interesting story of important achievements.

Recently, the American Ornithologists' Union (AOU) approved a change in the form of possessive bird names in its Check-list of North American Birds. *Rather than maintain the form in which names ending in s were followed simply by an apostrophe, the group dictated the addition of another s. Thus, the names used in this column—Lewis' woodpecker, Xantus' murrelet, Ross' gull, Ross' goose, and Harris' hawk—are now properly written as Lewis's woodpecker, Xantus's murrelet, Ross's gull and goose, and Harris's hawk.*

Form Follows Function: 1998

As we sit watching the birds at our backyard feeders, we are constantly amazed by the dexterity with which they use their beaks. A northern cardinal methodically extracts sunflower seeds from a tubular feeder and cracks them with its massive reddish bill. Empty hulls rain down as the handsome bird deftly separates and swallows the succulent kernels.

American goldfinches feed in a similar manner, but the process seems much more deliberate. With a smaller bill that imparts less leverage, the little finch must apply it more precisely. It manipulates each seed into position with its tongue in order to slice it open with the sharp edges of its short, triangular bill.

A Carolina chickadee, too, drops to the feeder and grabs a seed; however, it does not sit there to eat with the others. Instead, it flies up to a nearby tree with its prize. Holding the sunflower seed against a branch with its toes, it hammers it open with a few well-placed blows of its stubby little bill.

The cardinal, with its huge beak, is capable of cracking many large, hard-shelled seeds that the smaller goldfinch or chickadee cannot utilize. The latter two, however, are more adept at extracting tiny seeds or gleaning insect eggs or larvae from cracks and crevices.

Birds have evolved a seemingly endless array of beak sizes and shapes, each adapted to a particular feeding mechanism. The diet of each species dictates the form of its bill. A blue jay, for example, has what might be thought of as an all-purpose beak. Although it can crack seeds in the company of finches, it also captures large numbers of caterpillars and other insects, gulps down berries and small fruits, and even preys on small vertebrates or the eggs and nestlings of other birds.

Bird beaks vary from the long, slender rapiers that allow hummingbirds to probe deep within the throats of flowers to the sharp, wickedly hooked mandibles with which predatory hawks kill and dismember their prey.

Although the loggerhead shrike shares a familial relationship with the songbirds, it seems to be a hawk at heart. To facilitate its capture of small mammals and birds, as well as the insects, reptiles, and amphibians that supplement its diet, it, too, has a hooked, razor-sharp bill.

Despite their obvious differences, all of these beak forms arise in much the same way. Each is essentially a compact layer of specialized skin cells molded around the bony cores of the mandibles. The beak tissue comprises three distinct layers. Outwardly, there is a horny layer of the epidermis; inwardly, there is a softer layer where the epidermal cells multiply. Between the two are cells in which the keratin granules form. The hard outer sheath is normally renewed from below as it wears down through repeated use, but there are interesting variations on the theme.

The black skimmer feeds by flying just above the surface of the water with its lower mandible submerged. Such use would eventually reduce that portion of the bill to a stub, but the lower mandible grows much

Loggerhead shrike

more rapidly than the upper one, which suffers less wear. Skimmers kept in captivity and denied the opportunity to skim soon grow a lower mandible twice the length of the opposing one.

The beak of a duck is hard only at the tip, whereas the sides are relatively soft. Richly supplied with sensitive nerve endings, these pliable margins prove useful in detecting and filtering out small invertebrates and plant material from muddy water. The tactile sensors in the long bill of the woodcock, on the other hand, occur at the tip. There they aid in locating worms for which this aberrant shorebird probes deep in the soft, wet earth.

In some penguins, auks, and puffins, the hard keratin sheath thickens into pronounced scales, plates, or knobs. These persist only during the breeding season and are then shed immediately. They are presumably ornaments used in courtship, and their shedding seems to be a primitive characteristic reminiscent of reptilian scales, according to ornithologist Joel Carl Welty in his excellent text, *The Life of Birds.*

In many bird species, the hard material at the base of the upper mandible gives way to thick skin called the cere. Frequently this cere is brightly colored, as is the case in the parrots and birds of prey. The nostrils are usually located near the base of the upper mandible or in the cere, but again there are many variations among diverse species. Nocturnal kiwis of New Zealand, which find food primarily by scent, have their nostrils at the tips of their beaks, and the high-diving gannets have no external openings at all. They are essentially "mouth-breathers," a strategy that protects them as they hit the water with considerable force.

The evolution of this amazing array of beak types has allowed birds to feed in almost every conceivable ecological niche. The many shorebird species, for example, can feed at different water depths because of varying bill lengths, some probing more deeply in the sand or mud than others. The upswept beak of the avocet is wielded with scythelike movements along the bottom, stirring up tender morsels with the sediments, while the laterally compressed, sharp-edged beak of the oystercatcher serves as nature's original oyster knife.

Warblers glean insects from the foliage and bark of trees with their slender bills, while woodpeckers hammer away at the wood with their chisel-tipped beaks. Nighthawks and flycatchers catch insects in midair with their small but wide-gaping, bristle-fringed bills, and herons wield their sharp-pointed beaks like spears to impale fish.

Because birds have dedicated their forelimbs to flight, their beaks must also serve a variety of other purposes for which most creatures use their hands or front feet. With these amazing implements birds weave their nests, preen their feathers, excavate burrows, perform courtship displays, and defend themselves. There are almost as many variations as there are species, and in the case of birds' beaks, form definitely follows function.

The Eyes Have It: 1998

Many of us undoubtedly admire birds because of their bright colors and cheerful songs or because of their innate aerial abilities. One of the most remarkable attributes of birds, however, is the amazing acuteness of their vision. As author Joel Carl Welty wrote in his ornithological treatise, *The Life of Birds,* "The eye of the bird has reached a state of perfection found in no other animal."

Little escapes the notice of a hawk or eagle, and it has been claimed that a vulture can spot a carcass from more than ten thousand feet in the air. At that distance, the soaring vulture is not even visible to the human eye.

Most birds rely on their eyesight for finding food and for defense against potential predators. Although equipped with other faculties, they undoubtedly process more information about their surroundings through their eyes than through all other senses.

Birds have enormously large eyes for their size. Indeed, those of some hawks, eagles, and owls are actually bigger than the eyes of humans. Although our eyes make up less than 1 percent of the weight of our head, a starling's eyes account for about 15 percent. These enlarged orbs provide larger and sharper images, an invaluable asset to creatures that fly rapidly in and out among the trees, swooping to catch a running mouse or snatching an insect out of the air. The larger the eye, the greater its resolving power.

Not all of a bird's eye is visible; much is concealed behind the skull. In fact, the eyes of some birds have become so large that they cannot be moved in their sockets, and the bird must turn its head to follow a moving object. Nocturnal birds also have larger eyes than their diurnal counterparts, an obvious adaptation to weak illumination. Slowly, through natural selection, species that are active at

The keen, piercing eye of a Cooper's hawk

night have improved their ability to survey their surroundings under amazingly dark and difficult conditions.

The structure of the avian eye is much like that of a human one, but there are, of course, many variations. In general, birds have flattened eyeballs that make it possible for them to focus over the entire field of view. Everything is in focus at once, and this increased accommodation proves invaluable to a fast-moving bird whose landscape changes rapidly. Owls, however, have elongated, almost tubular eyeballs located well forward on their flattened faces. These allow sharp binocular vision for locating prey, but owls are unable to focus on close objects.

The colored iris of a bird's eye has extraordinary motility, opening spontaneously in dim light and closing down rapidly under brighter conditions. Although most species have round pupils, those of black skimmers close to oval slits, and those of the king penguin are square.

Birds typically have more photoreceptors in their retinas than do most other animals. The eye of a hawk was found to contain more than a million per square millimeter, giving it a visual acuity at least eight times that of humans. Even a little sparrow has four hundred thousand, twice the density of receptors in even the most sensitive portion of our own eyes.

Birds active during the daylight hours have more color-perceiving cones in their retinas; those active at night have an increased number of more light-sensitive rods. Not only are these cones and rods more numerous and tightly packed than in other vertebrates but conductive cells and nerve fibers are also unusually abundant. This means that almost all of what a bird sees is transmitted instantly to the vision centers of its brain.

Another unusual adaptation of avian eyes is the presence in many of the cones of tiny, colored oil droplets. These apparently increase the contrast of colored objects against their background and act like haze-piercing filters.

Birds have both upper and lower eyelids, but in addition there is a third eyelid called the nictitating membrane, which is used to keep out unusually bright light, to protect the eye from dust and dirt or physical injury, and, in some diving birds, to change the refractive index when under water. Transparent in most birds, this membrane is opaque in owls and more highly colored in a few other species. That of the magpie is white with a conspicuous orange spot that the bird displays during courtship or in hostile encounters with others. The inner surface of the nictitating membrane is covered with special cells bearing brushlike protrusions. These continually bathe the cornea with tears, cleansing and lubricating it.

A bird's field of view depends on three different factors: the placement of the eyes, their mobility, and the angle of view that each eye covers. The position of the eyes in a bird's head correlates closely with its feeding habits. Pigeons, for example, have eyes at the sides of their heads, a placement that gives them a visual field of about 340 degrees. Owls, on the other hand, have huge, immobile eyes placed frontally to provide binocular vision and depth perception when diving after prey. This gives them a total field of view of only 60 to 70 degrees. To compensate, owls have flexible necks that allow them to twist their heads around to survey their surroundings.

In the woodcock, which feeds by probing deeply into the mud with its long bill, the eyes have shifted backward and upward on the head so that they afford binocular vision to the rear. Better frontal vision would serve little purpose, but the woodcock can easily detect predators approaching from behind.

There are many different adaptations of the avian eye, each in keeping with the particular habits of the species. In general, however, birds look out on their world with remarkable acuity.

Feathers Make the Bird: 1996

It seems at first a simple and obvious observation: birds are covered with feathers. Indeed, no bird is without feathers, and no other kind of animal possesses them. Feathers define the avian world.

Considered in more detail, however, feathers are remarkably complex structures, varying in much more than size and color. There are several different types, each with a particular purpose. They protect the body from temperature extremes, water, the burning rays of the sun, and mechanical damage. They give buoyancy to waterbirds, serve as ornamentation and recognition marks in courtship and defense, and above all, make possible the power of flight.

Feathers probably evolved from reptilian scales, diverging into the highly complex structures we see today. Once fully formed, they lack living cells and are completely dead, receiving nothing more from the body except physical support. Welty, in his text, lists six commonly recognized types of feathers: vaned or contour, down, semiplume, filoplume, bristle, and powder down.

Most obvious are the vaned, or contour, feathers that cover a bird's body and give it its streamlined form. Those of the wings and tail that extend beyond the body and aid in flight are called the flight feathers.

The typical contour feather has a central shaft and a flat, flexible vane divided by the shaft into two webs. Each web, in turn, contains several hundred parallel filaments called barbs. Those next to the tip of the feather are usually stiff and flat; those near the base are loose and fluffy. Smaller barbules then hook together to keep the barbs aligned. According to Welty, "A single barb on a crane feather has about 600 barbules on each side, which means well over a million barbules for the entire feather." When a bird preens, it carefully hooks the barbules together, aligning the barbs and making the web work as a unit against the flow of air.

Down feathers lack these hooks and remain fluffy. Generally hidden beneath the contour feathers, particularly in waterfowl, they function primarily to conserve heat.

Intermediate in form, semiplume feathers typically occur along the sides of the abdomen and next to the large wing and tail feathers. They provide insulation, aid in flexibility, and increase the buoyancy of waterbirds.

Filoplumes are slender, whiplike shafts with only sparse barbs near the tip that apparently serve a sensory function in controlling feather movements.

Hairlike bristle feathers function as eyelashes in some species and filter dust from the nostrils of others. Rictal bristles surround the mouths of such aerial insect eaters as nighthawks and flycatchers,

Contour and down feathers

perhaps acting collectively as a supplemental net and funneling prey into the mouth.

Only the powder-down feathers grow continuously and are never molted. Found in dense patches on the underparts or flanks of herons or scattered on the bodies of such birds as hawks and parrots, their tips constantly disintegrate into a talclike powder. When distributed by preening, this powder helps waterproof and preserve the plumage.

Although primitive birds may have been evenly covered with feathers in a checkerboard pattern, only a few retain that arrangement today. The bodies of penguins, ostriches and their relatives, and a few others are uniformly cloaked in feathers, but such is not the case with most modern species. Instead, the feathers on most birds are distributed in scattered patches called feather tracts, with naked regions in between. Major tracts cover the crown, the spine, both sides of the breast, the upper wing, the thigh, and the remainder of the leg. One tract contains the tail feathers, and another holds the large flight feathers along the edge of the wing.

Feathers on the outer portion of the wing are called the primaries; those on the inner portion, the secondaries. Most songbirds possess nine functional primaries on each wing, and most other birds have ten. Grebes, storks, and flamingos, however, have eleven primaries. Secondaries vary in number from six for hummingbirds to forty on the enormously long wings of albatrosses.

Tail feathers, too, vary in number. Ordinarily there are ten or twelve, but anis have only eight, and the long, ornate tails of pheasants have twenty-four. Tail feathers are used mainly for steering and for maintaining balance in flight.

Because of the need for insulation against the cold, birds usually have more feathers in winter than during the summer months. A Carolina chickadee taken in February, for example, had 1,704 contour feathers, whereas another taken in June had only 1,140. Alaskan redpolls, according to Welty, have 31 percent heavier plumage in November than in July, and close relatives that spend the winter in different climates adapt their plumage to the temperature demands.

Even birds of the same species carry different numbers of feathers during the same season. Two female song sparrows collected in March had 2,208 and 2,093 feathers, respectively, and the differences may be even larger between the sexes.

As might be expected, body size is the single largest factor in determining the number of feathers a bird carries. A ruby-throated hummingbird was found to have 940 feathers; a tundra swan had 25,216. The tiny hummingbird, however, actually had more feathers per gram of body weight than the much larger swan, reflecting a proportionately greater heat loss from a smaller body.

On average, feathers make up about 6 percent of a bird's weight, although the contour feathers of a bald eagle were found to constitute 14 percent of its weight, more than twice as much as its skeleton.

As each delicate feather becomes worn, it loosens and is replaced by another growing beneath it. Adult birds commonly molt all or most of their feathers once a year, but many also have a partial molt before the breeding season. At this time, they may substitute brilliant colors useful in courtship for duller camouflage garb. Molt patterns, too, vary from species to species.

Thus, although we tend to think of feathers as parts of a simple covering for any bird, actual adaptations are far more complex. Feathers may define the bird, but there are seemingly endless variations on that theme.

A Rainbow of Color: 1997

One of the things that most attracts us to the world of birds is their remarkable variety of bright colors. Clearly, birds rank as the most vividly colored of all vertebrate animals, with the possible exception of the tropical coral-reef fishes. A flock of spring migrants, for example, resembles random fragments of a rainbow, with golden yellow prothonotary warblers, flame orange Baltimore orioles, brilliant scarlet tanagers, and iridescent indigo buntings. The male painted bunting combines hues of red, blue, and lime green in a tapestry of incomparable beauty.

Because of their ability to fly, birds are able to escape potential predators and can also nest in inaccessible sites, thereby freeing themselves to some extent from the need for dull camouflage plumage. Some, particularly the females, do wear cryptic colors suited to a reclusive life, but many others are more flamboyantly attired. Certainly they outshine the small rodents and other quadrupeds of comparable size.

These colors that birds adopt arise in two entirely different ways. Some are due to actual pigments; others stem from the internal structure of the feathers.

The high metabolic rate of birds produces an abundance of waste products that can be utilized in chemical pigmentation instead of being discarded. Melanins in the form of insoluble microscopic particles produce black, dull yellow, red, and brown. The amount and kind of melanin formed in the body apparently depend on the amount of various amino acids in the diet. The brighter yellow, orange, red, and violet colors, on the other hand, come from a wide variety of complex, fat-soluble pigments called lipochromes.

Costa's Hummingbird

Unlike the pigmented colors, structural colors depend either on interference phenomena or on the scattering of shorter wavelengths by small particles within the feather. If the feather is reduced to a fine powder, thereby destroying its microscopic structure, those colors no longer exist.

Interference colors are like those of a soap bubble, in which different wavelengths of light are refracted or reflected from thin layers within the tiny barbs and barbules in such a way that certain wavelengths are reinforced while others are nullified. We notice such effects in the iridescent beauty of a peacock's tail or in the sparkling gorget of a hummingbird, and the hues depend on the angle of the light. Viewed with the sun behind the observer, the feathers shimmer with vibrant colors; lit from another angle, they appear dark and lifeless.

Still other feathers contain tiny particles that scatter the shorter wavelengths. Because only that portion of the incident light will be reflected, the feathers appear blue when illuminated from any angle. The same phenomenon, called Tyndall scattering, is also responsible for the apparent blue color of the sky. There are actually very few blue pigments in nature, and strange as it may seem, the familiar plumage of the blue jay, bluebird, or indigo bunting is not really blue at all. The beauty of this plumage is literally in the eye of the beholder.

Our Life with Birds

Even a single feather may contain different pigments and structural modifications. Red and yellow compounds commonly produce orange. Green is often the result of a pigmented yellow sheath on top of structural blue. The more densely packed the pigment granules, the darker the color, whereas a complete lack of pigment results in a white feather.

Once the feather is fully formed, circulation is cut off, and it can no longer receive new pigments. Its color may still change, however, usually by fading in the sunlight or by abrasion. Thus, the pale pink breasts that some gulls acquire during the breeding season quickly fade to white as light-sensitive red porphyrins are exposed to the rays of the sun. The nuptial black bib of the common house sparrow results from wear of the light-tipped breast feathers through the winter, and similar erosion of a starling's plumage trims away light feather tips to produce a darker appearance.

Heavily pigmented feathers are more resistant to wear than unpigmented ones, and for this reason, many of our white birds, such as gulls, snow geese, whooping cranes, white ibises, and white pelicans, have black wing tips. The particles of melanin impart additional strength where it is needed most.

Diet can play a significant role in the feather color of many birds. Flamingos normally lose their distinctive red or pink plumage in captivity, but zoos have discovered the color can be restored by feeding them shrimp and other crustaceans. Similarly, captive canaries gradually change from yellow to vivid orange in successive molts if fed red peppers.

With each bird species, there is also the possibility of abnormal coloration due to a variety of factors. Lack of pigment causes albinism, whereas too much melanin gives rise to darker, melanistic plumage. Other individuals may have an excess of red or yellow pigments that is reflected in the hue of their feathers. Much remains to be learned about the origins of avian color. The net result of all these combinations, however, is a varied and beautiful feathered palette that birds use in a wide variety of ways.

Albinism in Birds: 1989

There was something strange about the pudgy little bird walking slowly through the thicket at the Houston Audubon Society's Louis Smith Sanctuary in High Island this spring. It had the bobbing, hesitant gait of an ovenbird, a ground-dwelling warbler, but there was too much white in the plumage for this familiar species.

As we crept cautiously closer, we could see that it was indeed an ovenbird, its rusty crown bordered with black, and its white underparts boldly streaked with brown. Most striking, however, was a wide white collar completely encircling the neck, a mark not shown in any field guide. The collar was the result of partial albinism, a moderately common occurrence in birds. The normal pigments were simply lacking in those feathers.

As we watched this strange migrant, other birders approached and told us they had seen another partial albino ovenbird earlier in the day. That one had the white extending up both sides of the face, clearly in a different pattern than on the bird we were watching. Against enormous odds, there were apparently two aberrant ovenbirds in the small tract of woods that day.

A few days later, while birding in the Sabal Palm Sanctuary near Brownsville in Texas' Lower Rio Grande Valley, we chanced upon yet another such genetic oddity. This was a black-and-white warbler with a snowy white head; the normal black crown stripes were present only as small, scattered flecks of pale gray. There, in the presence of subtropical birds we seldom see, and in a wave of migrants as colorful as blackburnian warblers and rose-breasted grosbeaks, we stood for many minutes and watched the pale-headed warbler as it clambered up and down the slender branches of a tepeguaje tree.

We enjoy discovering the unusual, the little tricks of nature, as much as we enjoy the enormously varied and more dependable beauties of the world around us. We have delighted in a piebald cotton rat, its abnormal white pelage spotted sparingly with brown, and a shocking-pink katydid or blue frog. Most of these anomalies do not fare well in their hostile, predatory world, for the millennia of adaptation have not prepared them for existence outside the normal parameters of their kin. Those that do survive, however, prove even more interesting than those assembled from a perfect set of genes.

True and total albinism, where the animal lacks dark pigment completely, is fairly rare in nature. In fully albino birds, all the feathers are white; the skin and eyes, pink. There are other degrees of albinism in which the intensity of the color is reduced and the bird is very pale, or in which the pigment is completely absent from either eyes, skin, or feathers, but not from all three.

Partial albinism is moderately common in birds. Only some of the feathers are involved, and the result is an individual with white feathers set against the normal color pattern. The darker colors—black and brown—seem to be more easily replaced by white than are the paler red or yellow.

Several years ago, on the grounds of the Armand Bayou Nature Center near Houston, we encountered an American robin with large white spots over most of its body and a head that was mainly white. Although an enormous flock of other robins foraged nearby, this striking bird fed alone, a social outcast spurned by its peers. *(We watched another, somewhat similarly marked robin at Armand Bayou in the spring of 2003. That bird was liberally flecked with white and had a white breast.)*

Aberrant, partial albino black-and-white warbler

We have photographed both common grackles and house sparrows with abnormal white feathers, and one red-winged blackbird in a large flock near Corpus Christi had a left wing that was almost entirely white. Amazingly, another bird in the same flock had a white right wing.

Virtually every birder has seen variations on this theme. Ted Eubanks told us of an unusual American redstart he captured for banding: it was entirely white except for yellow patches in the wings and tail. And, at Aransas National Wildlife Refuge, visitors delighted in a male yellow-headed blackbird that was, instead, a yellow-headed whitebird. Nature is full of such fascinating tricks that add variety and interest to days afield along our nature trails.

Flight Defines the Avian World: 1996

One of the things we most admire about birds is their ability to fly. Who among us has not watched a hawk soar effortlessly on rising thermals or observed a flock of warblers flitting from tree to tree without some degree of envy. The power of flight provides the avian world with an enormous advantage over earthbound creatures. Birds can forage over much larger areas and flee quickly and effectively from danger. Flight also allows many birds to migrate thousands of miles, taking advantage of two vastly different habitats at different seasons of the year.

This aerial prowess, however, does not come without a price. Nearly every portion of a bird's body has been modified for flight; every aspect of its biology is finely tuned to accommodate this taxing mode of transportation.

It has been necessary, for example, for birds to become lighter in order to take to the skies. Some of the bones common to most other vertebrates have been eliminated; others are fused together. Many are "pneumatized," or filled with air spaces, although they retain their strength by being highly mineralized and having reinforcing struts that run throughout the hollow spaces.

The long, bony tails of reptiles, from which birds apparently evolved, have been lost. They would have been intolerably heavy and contribute little to the flight process. Similarly, the jaws and teeth, which are among the heaviest structures in other animals, have given way to tough, horny beaks.

Power is generated in the breast muscles, which make up a third or more of the body weight of fast-flying birds. These muscles have been shifted ventrally to improve aerodynamic balance, and the muscles of the back have been greatly reduced.

Birds have highly efficient circulatory and respiratory systems to supply the flight muscles with fuel and oxygen. The heart is much larger than that of reptiles or mammals of comparable size, and the lungs are connected to a series of air sacs that spread throughout the body, some even extending into the hollow bones.

Birds need enormous amounts of energy and have higher metabolic rates than those of most other animals. The tiny hummingbird, with its rapid, darting flight and its ability to hover, probably has the highest metabolism of any vertebrate and must feed almost constantly to fuel its internal fires.

In order to achieve this metabolic rate, birds consume high-energy foods, including seeds, fruits, nectar, insects, and other animals, resulting in high concentrations of glucose in their blood. To conserve the heat they generate, birds have reduced or lost entirely such heat-radiating projections as external ears and fleshy tails. Their bodies are swathed in insulating feathers.

Because of their speed and the necessity to react quickly, birds have highly refined nervous systems. Their brains are relatively large and complex, and they have sacrificed much of their sense of smell and taste for visual acuity. The eye of a bird has reached a degree of perfection found in no other animal.

The basic transformation of the forelimbs into wings limits their use for other functions. Many mammals use their front legs for holding and carrying, but birds must manage with their bills and feet.

In cross section, a bird's wing is similar to that of an airplane. Convex above and concave below, it has a thicker, rounded leading edge and a thin trailing edge. Because air flows more rapidly over the upper surface, there is a resulting upward lift.

Ruby-throated hummingbird

Flight feathers change shape throughout the wing beat. The trailing edge of each feather is broader and more flexible than the leading edge, and the vane twists, forcing air backward and producing a forward thrust. To fly faster, the bird flaps faster or more powerfully, making the wing feathers twist more and thereby increasing the thrust.

On the upward stroke, the wrist flexes to fold the outer part of the wing and separate the primaries. This lets air stream through without pushing the bird down. A small backward sweep gives an additional forward push.

During takeoff or when hovering, the bird loses the lift created by air flowing over the wings. It then moves its wings in exaggerated sweeping movements, like the rotor of a helicopter, to generate added lift. The takeoff demands an enormous amount of energy. Most birds spring into the air and fan their tails to deflect the airstream downward, beating their wings more deeply than in level flight. The loud wing noises that doves and other species produce in takeoff is actually the sound of the wings hitting each other above the body in an attempt to gain more lift.

Our Life with Birds

Birds with weak legs, such as swifts, or those with legs set far back on their bodies, cannot jump to take off. Instead, they may drop from a perch or ledge, gaining momentum and lift as they spread their wings. Some ducks can spring directly into flight from the surface of the water, but others must run flapping across the surface until they reach flight speed. As with an airplane, it is helpful if they can take off into a headwind.

Landing, too, can be a precarious operation. The bird must slow down and lose altitude without losing control and crashing. Fanning the tail and changing to deeper wing beats provide extra lift, and some birds tip from side to side so that air spills between the widely spread wing feathers.

Steering in flight is accomplished by subtle movements of the wings. By flexing or extending one wing, the bird changes the lift and begins to turn. The tail is also twisted from the horizontal to reinforce these wing effects.

In order to conserve energy, many bird species employ a flap-and-glide style, coasting whenever possible after gaining momentum, flapping again to gain altitude. The ultimate in fuel conservation is the soaring flight many larger birds adopt. Utilizing updrafts and thermals, they may sail for hours on end with little expenditure of energy.

Bird flight is enormously complex, and various species use different methods to meet their individual needs. Whatever their techniques, they are marvelous examples of biological engineering at its best.

The Flightless Few: 1996

Although the power of flight enables birds to migrate long distances, forage over large areas, and escape from potential predators, it is an extremely expensive process physiologically, requiring many special adaptations and large expenditures of energy. It also places severe limits on a bird's weight and dictates a specialized body structure.

When the advantages of flight no longer compensate for the enormous cost, wings may atrophy or disappear. About forty species of flightless birds exist today around the world, and many others have become extinct in recent times. All are thought to have descended from flying ancestors.

In general, flightlessness is associated with geographic isolation and the absence of mammalian predators. Many such birds inhabit remote islands with few serious threats, and others rely on nocturnal or secretive habits. Some ornithologists suggest that wings may even be a handicap to island-dwelling birds, increasing their chances of being blown out to sea and drowned during raging storms.

The penguins of the Southern Hemisphere form the largest group of flightless birds. They have abandoned the skies to gain remarkable prowess in the water, and their wings have become thin, rigid paddles. Using a different wing beat, in which the entire flipper twists, they literally fly through the waters of their chosen marine environments and dive to astonishing depths. With weight no longer a primary concern, penguins can also put on thick layers of insulating fat to keep them warm, even in frigid, ice-laden Antarctic seas. The largest living penguin, the emperor, weighs more than sixty pounds.

The ostriches, rheas, cassowaries, and emus have likewise lost the ability to fly. Their flattened breastbones lack the keel necessary to anchor strong flight muscles, and their small wings are useful mainly for balance as they run or for sheltering their broods. Ostrich feathers have lost the barbules that link them together so that the vanes are loose and fluffy. These birds, called ratites, compensate for their flightlessness with their large size, keen eyesight, aggressiveness, and speed afoot. Ostriches can run at nearly forty miles an hour and deliver wicked kicks with their powerful legs and two-toed feet.

Closely related but much smaller are the kiwis of New Zealand. Short-legged and about the size of chickens, they live secretively in the forests, hiding in burrows and emerging at night to feed on earthworms and insects. Kiwis rely largely on their keen sense of smell and have poorer eyesight than most other birds. Because their soft, barbless feathers resemble fur, these wingless birds have been called "honorary mammals" in a land where there are no large native mammals.

Many species of rails have become flightless, particularly those established on remote oceanic islands. Typically dull colored and secretive, they are often nocturnal and slink quietly away through the reeds or marsh grasses when disturbed.

New Zealand is also home to a flightless parrot, the kakapo, and to the gallinule-like takahe. The latter was once thought to be extinct, only to be rediscovered in 1948 in a remote mountain valley.

Flightless steamer ducks live in the coastal waters of South America's Patagonia. Their wings are too small for flight, but they use them as paddles to swim strongly on the surface of the water.

A flightless cormorant inhabits the Galápagos Islands off the coast of Ecuador, and New Caledonia is home to the rare kagu, which sleeps in crevices or under tree roots during the day and forages at night.

Magellanic penguin

Because most of these flightless birds evolved in the absence of large predators, they are extremely vulnerable to human intrusion and the introduction of alien animals. Dogs, cats, pigs, and rats have all taken their toll of island birds.

The famous dodo of Mauritius, for example, rapidly succumbed to human pressure and disappeared in the 1680s, when sailing ships invaded its island home and sailors found the tasty, pigeonlike meat a welcome addition to their stores. Similarly, the great auk was lost forever in 1844, when the last birds were killed near Iceland. These large, goose-sized alcids, whose present-day relatives retain the ability to fly, once inhabited islands from St. Kilda off Scotland to Canada's Gulf of St. Lawrence; however, their vulnerability made them easy victims of fishermen seeking food and bait.

The Laysan rail was extirpated by rats from a World War II ship; the last Wake Island rails were killed and eaten by the Japanese garrison.

New Zealand's Stephen Island wren is believed to have been the only modern-day flightless songbird. It also holds the dubious distinction of being the only species to be discovered and extirpated by the same creature. Revealed to science when the lighthouse keeper's cat brought home one of the birds it had caught, the wren apparently vanished in 1894 under the persistent pressure of that same skilled hunter.

Sacrificing the ability to fly through the air allows many other avian adaptations. It enables ostriches to grow to enormous size and to run with the large mammals of the African plains, and it allows penguins to perfect their aquatic skills. But flightlessness also makes island birds vulnerable to changing conditions and new predators with which they are unprepared to cope. Intrusion into their isolated domains is driving many unique forms of avian life toward a fate already suffered by the moa and the dodo.

5

Birds Being Birds

The daily antics of even our most common birds provide fruitful fields of study for ornithologists and behavioral scientists, as well as countless hours of enjoyment for observant birders. Each species, indeed every individual bird, has its own characteristic habits and routines and its own unique personality. Bird-watching, in the best sense of the term, reveals intimate details of the life of birds, during their waking hours and even while they are asleep.

Bathing Beauties: 1985

Preceded by a chorus of raucous cries that heralds their approach, a small group of blue jays swirls into the backyard in search of the handout they know to be there. After consuming large quantities of sunflower seeds and bread crumbs, the garrulous birds next move to the birdbath where, pushing and shoving like small boys in a farm pond, they proceed to bathe. Dipping their heads, they raise them quickly, throwing a cascade of droplets over their backs. This is then followed by a vigorous beating of wings, splashing torrents of water everywhere.

Each bird employs the same bathing sequence, as if it has learned its lessons from a book on avian hygiene. Indeed, this is virtually the case, for the urge to bathe and the motions employed seem to be instincts that are genetically derived.

Blue jay

Baths over, the jays perch in the branches of an oak tree overhead and begin to preen. First shaking the water from their wings, they fluff out their feathers and carefully arrange them again, drawing each feather through the beak to smooth it and remove the remaining dirt. This process also rehooks all the tiny barbules that keep the feathers flat yet stiff enough to repel water and allow flight. Author John Terres, in *The Audubon Society Encyclopedia of North American Birds,* calls preening "the basic and most important single act that a bird performs in the care of its feathers."

All aquatic birds and most land birds take water baths of one kind or another. We have watched as whole flocks of gulls bathed together in a small sun-warmed tidal pool along the beach. It was, we suppose, the avian equivalent of a hot-tub party.

Hummingbird visitors to our yard in late summer dart repeatedly into the path of the lawn sprinkler, hovering in the spray before perching to dry and preen. The resident northern mockingbirds rub their plumage vigorously against the leaves of a mulberry tree soaked by the same sprinkler, bathing in the foliage as they would after a rain or heavy dew. During hot weather, bathing undoubtedly provides welcome cooling, but the prime motivation seems to be to clean the plumage and to facilitate the preening and oiling of the feathers.

Smaller passerine birds bathe hurriedly with vigorous and continuous splashing, perhaps because it is a time of increased vulnerability to predators and thus a process to be completed quickly. Hawks, on the other hand, have been seen to lie motionless in the water for longer periods of time, evidently enjoying the cooling respite.

The instinctive nature of bathing is illustrated by the fact that four-week-old goshawks have been observed to go through the same motions on bare ground that they would use while splashing in the water. Young hawks of other species raised in captivity also have attempted to bathe on a shiny piece of plastic, using all the typical postures and movements.

Some ground-dwelling birds, particularly those that live in deserts where moisture is not readily available, bathe not in water but in the dust, a medium used by several birds of prey, sparrows, and others in addition to the more normal water baths. The dusting bird usually squats or lies prostrate in a sunny spot and forms a body-size hollow in which it sifts dust or sand through its plumage by fluttering its wings and rolling around with feathers fluffed. Presumably dust, like water, serves to clean debris and oil from the feathers and probably helps to eliminate external parasites. Preening usually follows, as with a water bath.

Sunbathing is not an exclusively human pastime, for birds also like to "catch some rays." Venturing out into the hot summer sunshine, a blue jay or cardinal may raise its crown feathers, spread its wings and tail, and lie immobile for several minutes. So, too, the Inca doves in our backyard, which often roll onto one side and raise a wing to the penetrating rays.

In some cases, birds sunbathe on relatively cool days, perhaps merely enjoying the solar warmth. The roadrunner, for example, raises the feathers on its back to allow the sun to warm the dark skin below. Frequently, however, the surface on which birds rest to sunbathe is almost unbearably hot, and they open their beaks and flutter their throats—the avian equivalent of panting—in an obvious effort to keep cool. The sunshine seems almost to trigger an involuntary bathing reflex.

It has been suggested that in addition to providing heat, the sunshine may stimulate production of vitamin D. It may also cause ectoparasites to abandon their hold or to move to places where they can be more readily reached and removed.

Whether birds choose to bathe in a pool of water or backyard birdbath, in roadside dust, or in a bright ray of sunshine, preening invariably follows. It is important in the care of the feathers on which birds' lives depend. In this case, cleanliness is not only next to godliness, it is absolutely essential.

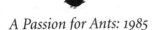

A Passion for Ants: 1985

Although bathing and preening are vital if birds are to remain warm and dry, with their feathers in good condition, another instinctive activity may also be related to feather maintenance. This is the bizarre behavior called "anting."

Audubon, in his *Ornithological Biography* of 1831, was the first to write of this strange habit. He witnessed wild turkeys rolling in ant nests and suggested they were doing so "to clear their growing feathers of the loose scales and prevent ticks and other vermin from attacking them, these insects being unable to bear the odor of the earth in which the ants have been."

In 1876, another American ornithologist, Abbott Frazar, described the behavior of his pet crow as it stood on an anthill and permitted ants to crawl over it, presumably "to carry away the troublesome vermin."

More than two hundred bird species have been added to the list of those that practice anting, according to John Terres in *The Audubon Society Encyclopedia of North American Birds*. The observations extend around the world. At least twenty-four species of ants are utilized by various birds, and some forty other kinds of substitute materials are also rubbed into avian plumage. The instinct is far from a simple one.

Anting behavior may be exhibited in either an active or a passive form. In the latter, as with Frazar's crows and Audubon's turkeys, the bird spreads its wings and stretches out over an anthill, letting the aroused insects crawl through its ruffled feathers.

In active anting, the bird grasps an ant in its beak and strokes its feathers with the insect, sometimes jabbing the ant repeatedly and forcefully into its plumage. The underparts of the body, wings, and tail are most frequently anointed. In its seemingly ecstatic contor-

Our Life with Birds

tions, the bird may even step on its own wing or tail and tumble over on the ground. The ants used in this ritual are frequently those species that possess pungent or acidic body fluids. Sometimes they are discarded after anting; sometimes they are eaten.

Although ants are most often used, birds have been observed substituting such items as beetles, snails, lemon or orange peel, raw onion, coffee, soapsuds, sour berries, hair tonic, cigarette butts, and burning matches. In Pennsylvania, according to Terres, a woman watched grackles coming to her English walnut trees over a period of fifteen years. Picking holes in the hulls before the nuts were ripe, the birds dipped in their bills and then proceeded to preen their feathers with the sticky juice. Similarly, grackles in Wisconsin used mothballs placed in a vegetable garden to keep rabbits from the tender greens.

Most of the ant substitutes are acidic, presumably serving the same purpose as the formic acid exuded by the hymenopterous insects. In one experiment where a starling was offered a boiled, acid-free ant, it tried it once and then discarded it. Normal acid-producing ants were used repeatedly.

The instinctive nature of anting behavior was nicely demonstrated in experiments with starlings. Hand-raised young first ate the ants offered them, but at thirty-seven days of age they began anting instead, obviously with no parental guidance.

Clearly, the instinct for the anting behavior is very strong, but the benefits from the process remain uncertain. Various authors have proposed some of the following explanations: acidic fluids from ants or their substitutes serve as insecticides to kill or repel external parasites; the fluids relieve itching or act as medicinal tonics on the skin; and ant fluids provide physical protection for the feathers, perhaps supplementing the oil from the birds' own preen glands.

Reviewing all the data, E. F. Potter concluded that anting displays coincide most frequently with seasonal molt. She, and several other scientists, thus assert that the chemicals may be effective in soothing skin irritation and help in the maintenance of new feathers.

Whatever the reason for the strange behavior, many of our common

European starling "anting"

birds display a passion for anting. A cardinal sprawled on an anthill or a blue jay rubbing ants under its wings is just following a genetic urge for a formic-acid rinse.

Perchance to Sleep: 1990

It was late on a rare subfreezing afternoon, and we were watching a flock of Inca doves feeding on scattered seed in our backyard in Baytown, Texas. Three of the dainty little doves then flew up to perch on a tree branch and crowded close together. Others soon joined the trio, all packing in as tightly as space permitted. One late arrival landed atop the pile and snuggled down between two others, actually perching on their backs. A total of nine birds sat huddled together, eyes closed and feathers fluffed against the cold. We do not know if they actually slept or if they were merely resting, conserving precious energy against the chill north wind. They departed before dark, probably for a more sheltered nook, where they may well have congregated in similar fashion for the night.

Our Life with Birds

The sleeping habits of birds are as varied as their daytime foraging, courtship, or nesting behavior. Some establish communal roosts; others remain strictly to themselves, "Far from the madding crowd's ignoble strife," as Thomas Gray so elegantly wrote. Most, of course, are diurnal and sleep at night, but a few nocturnal species sleep by day. The nighttime habits of many birds are virtually unknown, for they are extremely difficult to observe.

Alexander Skutch, in *Birds Asleep,* treats this varied behavior in intimate detail. A longtime resident of Costa Rica, Skutch is the author of several excellent volumes, including a long-awaited field guide to Costa Rican birds. He has been aptly described as a "renowned philosopher of natural history."

"The sleeping habits of birds are so intimately related to their social life that knowledge of one may shed light upon the other. To find a safe place to sleep is no less important to birds than to find a safe place for their nests," says Skutch. "To know how they pass the more obscure half of their lives is necessary to round out our picture of their habits."

Oceanic birds, for example, have various ways of coping with the night. The auks, petrels, shearwaters, and albatrosses spend most of their life at sea. Although they are frequently active by night as well as by day, they apparently sleep on the water. Some penguins remain at sea except to nest; others return to shore each night to sleep. Because the plumage of the cormorants becomes quickly waterlogged, those highly aquatic birds must also return to land to dry their wings.

Most gulls and terns forage near the coasts and roost at night on shore. However, the sooty tern is not known to visit land except during the nesting season. Strangely, it is also a species whose plumage readily absorbs water, according to Skutch, and "could hardly survive an hour on the surface of the sea." Thus, it apparently sleeps on the wing and "remains continuously airborne, probably beating its wings slowly while it dozes." Frigatebirds presumably share this behavior, continuously soaring over the oceans of the world, sleeping as they fly and returning to land only to lay their eggs and rear their young.

Geese and cranes frequently roost on ponds at night, where they are less accessible to roving predators, and fly off to feed in surrounding fields the next morning. Sandpipers doze on mudflats and sandy shores, heads tucked under their wings, each with one leg drawn up into the belly plumage to minimize heat loss.

A few birds roost in large communal flocks, perhaps deriving some safety from predators by their sheer numbers. It has also been suggested that nighttime roosts may serve as "information centers" from which some birds follow others to newly discovered food supplies.

Some mated birds roost in pairs; others, singly. Some sleep in the nest with their young and may even lead them back at night after they have fledged.

Woodpeckers, of course, chisel holes that can serve as night roosts as well as nests, and other birds may appropriate abandoned woodpecker holes as their own. However, few species actually build structures for sleeping. "By molting," notes Skutch, "a bird might be said to build itself a new dwelling every year. The bird's feather-house has a water-repellent roof and sides." And that, for many, is enough to see them safely through the chilliest of nights.

Magnificent frigatebird with throat pouch inflated

Our Life with Birds

A World Filled with Song: 1985

It is well past midnight when we are awakened from a deep sleep by a persistent sound. Light from the full moon is streaming in the window of our bedroom, and we lie quietly listening. It is a birdsong, loud yet melodious, each phrase repeated two or three times with seemingly no end to the varied repertoire. One of our resident mockingbirds is inspired by the moonlight and the imminent spring to assert his claim to our front yard. We smile at the intrusion and go back to sleep, lulled by the melodies of a master musician.

Our natural world is filled with avian music, songs that all too often we do not stop to hear. We go about with our ears tuned to the refrains of the throbbing, pulsating city or to Bach, Willie Nelson, or Cyndi Lauper—depending on our musical tastes—with little regard for the clear whistles of the cardinals or the cheerful chatter of the chickadees and titmice.

Some of our most vivid and treasured memories include the dawn song of a hermit thrush on the rim of the Grand Canyon and the serenade of a tiny hooded warbler one morning in the bottomland forests of deep East Texas. We always stop and look up in delight to the cries of geese streaming past in ragged skeins or to the wonderful rolling calls of sandhill cranes overhead. As clearly as if it happened yesterday, we remember resting our paddles on the thwarts of a canoe and drifting in silence on a Minnesota lake to listen at sunset to the vespers of the veeries.

Not all birdsongs, of course, are as pleasing to our ears. Outside our door as we work is a flock of common grackles, each trying to outdo the others with a strange assortment of squawks, shrieks, and rattles. They compete with their own unique music not for record sales or Grammy Awards but for perpetuation of their genes. By singing, they communicate within the flock, claim territories for feeding or nesting, and seek their mates.

In spring, a bird's song might say to others of the species, "I've staked my claim here, and I'm king of the hill." With much posturing and flashing of wings and tail, males sing and show off to attract the females. Pair bonds are forged and strengthened by song.

Birdsongs are useful, too, to birders and to ornithologists who study avian biology. Our common eastern meadowlark, for example, looks very much like the western meadowlark that occasionally strays to the Texas coast. It is difficult to tell them apart in the field solely by their plumage. Their songs, however, are very different, and the bird-watcher who is also a bird listener can readily separate the two.

Such is also the case with many of our small flycatchers of the genus *Empidonax*. So similar are they in plumage that they are frequently identified in the field only on the basis of their songs. Two species, the willow and alder flycatchers, were until recently considered to be a single species, called Traill's flycatcher. Although they are almost indistinguishable in appearance, they have different songs. And because the song is an important part of courtship activity, the two apparently do not interbreed, a factor considered by ornithologists in describing them as separate species.

Neither of us has, unfortunately, a good ear for birdsongs, nor do we seem able to remember the sometimes slight variations that distinguish one from another. However, we have seen time and time again the value of birding by ear.

Many years ago, we birded for a few days in the southeastern corner of Arizona, a "hot spot" that harbors many Mexican species found nowhere else in the United States. Our companion was from Delaware and had never been west of the Mississippi, but he had a keen musical ear and had carefully studied the recordings of western birds before our trip. Rick was repeatedly able to locate the rarities we sought by pinpointing their songs, and he saved us valuable time by recognizing the sounds of common birds we might otherwise have followed up and down the mountainsides.

More recently, in remote Corcovado National Park in Costa Rica, John was in the field with noted wildlife artist Larry McQueen. Having birded extensively in the tropics, Larry was familiar with many of the songs and could frequently identify birds long before they were seen. Recording their songs on a small tape recorder and playing them back, he lured the singers out into the open where they could be pho-

tographed at close range for
future use in paintings.

This use of recordings is a
powerful technique for at-
tracting birds, but one that
must be tempered with cau-
tion. We see no problem in
using it in a remote location
to attract a bird for one-time
study or identification or to
show it once to a field-trip
group. However, this can be
too much of a good thing
when dozens of people pursue a single bird over and over

Eastern meadowlark

again. In that case, repeated playing of taped songs may actually drive
the bird from its territory or distract it from its normal routine. The
method has deservedly fallen into disrepute with responsible birders.

Whether you use birdsongs as a key to finding and identifying
the various species or simply enjoy them for their pleasing sounds,
it is well worth stopping to listen. Some of nature's best musicians
live right in our own backyards.

They Will Do It Their Way: 1991

Birds, like people, have their individual personalities. Many are highly
social creatures, but some are typically loners that choose to avoid
the company of others. Each bird has certain territorial requirements
that vary with the season and the circumstance. On the nesting
grounds, for example, mated pairs normally keep to themselves and
chase intruders from their territories. When the species live in
crowded colonies and feed together in communal areas, as do the
coastal gulls and terns, an individual territory may be only as large
as the distance the incubating bird can reach. Any bird venturing into
that hemisphere, however, is likely to be severely punished.

A pair of eagles, on the other hand, might stake claim to several square miles over which they reign. This is their personal hunting ground and assures an adequate food supply for them and their hatchlings. Most other species are free to come and go, but the rulers exclude potential competitors.

Territorial behavior has little to do with size. Purple martins choose to nest together in busy apartment complexes, but no tiny yet pugnacious hummingbird would allow another of its species to build on the same tree branch.

These barriers break down when the nesting season is concluded, and many species flock together in migration. Shorebirds blend in enormous flocks, and hundreds of hawks swirl on thermals overhead as if in an avian chorus line. There is little competition except for the shared battle against inclement weather and the interminable miles that stretch ahead.

Birds set up feeding territories, too, and defend them almost as rigorously as their nests. A hummingbird will guard its own favored feeder or plot of flowers; a mockingbird might patrol its favorite fruit-laden tree long after its young are grown and gone.

On a recent trip through southern Texas with the Spring Branch Science Center, we had many chances to observe the interactions of various birds, and such encounters can be every bit as fascinating as adding new species to a list. The habits of the birds and their relationships with each other give them personality and make them more interesting.

Barn swallows lined the wires along our route, interrupting their migration to rest and feed. They nestled close together on their perches, carrying on seemingly pleasant conversations as they sat, for there appeared to be no competition there. When they left the wires to feed, they coursed the fields one by one, each seeking its own space in which to hunt.

Scissor-tailed flycatchers, too, lined the fences in astonishing numbers, sometimes a hundred or more within a quarter mile. They did not sit as close, however, as the swallows, but kept their distance from their neighbors as if never formally introduced. In flycatcher

Least grebe

fashion, each was watching for flying insects from its perch. The territories were small but well defined.

In the thorn-scrub woodlands of Santa Ana National Wildlife Refuge, we encountered a small flock of tufted titmice *(now separated again as the black-crested titmouse)*, blue-gray gnatcatchers, ruby-crowned kinglets, and several species of warblers, all feeding together through the treetops. Such associations might seem at first unusual, but the behavior seems to be the rule. A cooperative effort is probably more efficient in defense and also prevents foraging birds from searching areas already covered by others.

On a nearby pond, tiny least grebes were not as sociable; each kept its distance as it dove repeatedly for food. With lowered head and ruffled feathers, yellow eyes gleaming fiercely, one even steamed after a pied-billed grebe twice its size and drove it off. Presumably, the resident least grebe had no intention of sharing its territory with a newcomer, no matter what its size.

Like people, birds are individuals. Watching their behavior and discovering their personalities and idiosyncrasies can add a great deal to the joy of birding.

6

How Birds Rear Their Young

The urge to procreate must certainly rank as one of the most powerful driving forces in the animal world, and birds are by no means immune to this overwhelming stimulus. During the breeding season, most of their energies are channeled toward courtship, defense of territory, nest building, and the rearing of their young. Each species has unique methods to assure the continuation of its genetic lineage.

Birds build an amazing variety of nests to house their eggs and young. Some are solid fortresses against intruders, whereas others are carefully concealed to avoid predation. Many birds lay their eggs directly on the ground, relying on camouflage for protection. These individual preferences in nest construction help to determine the number, shape, and color of the eggs as well as the state of development of the newly hatched chicks. Their nesting habits are intricately intertwined with other aspects of their fascinating biology.

What Price Love?: 1989

It was late in the afternoon when we reached Lake Corpus Christi State Park and pulled into our favorite campsite well away from the crowd. We quickly set up camp and were seated at a picnic table having supper when we heard a strange noise, a repeated "thump, thump, thump," coming from the other side of our Volkswagen van. Edging slowly around the vehicle, we discovered a bright red male cardinal attacking his image in the side mirror. Perching on the window, he then flew directly at the mirror, hitting it with his chest and raking claws. Fluttering for a moment, he landed on top of the mirror, looked down at it with seeming curiosity, and then flew back down to repeat the process time and time again.

We watched in amusement for a few minutes and then wandered off to the lakeshore to enjoy the sunset across the water. When we returned, the bird was still at it, and he persisted until dark, determined to drive away the intruder who had so rudely invaded his territory.

The next morning, we awakened at first light to the whistled song of a cardinal in a tree nearby, and the thumping then started again. Still drowsy, John crawled out and pulled a small canvas bag over the mirror, hoping to get a few more minutes of sleep. To no avail, however, for the thumping quickly began again, this time from the mirror on the other side. The cardinal had discovered yet another adversary that must be vanquished.

Had we not been moving on, we would have changed our campsite to give its rightful tenants respite. Obviously, this site had been reserved by a cardinal couple, and the male could ill afford to spend all his time defending it against an unyielding apparition he could not defeat.

Northern cardinal

Continuing on to the Rio Grande Valley in deep South Texas, we encountered other birds engaged in the business of courtship and the establishment of their territories. With apologies to Tennyson, it is not just a young man's fancy that turns to thoughts of love in spring. The birds become equally enamored and may look just as silly in the process.

At Bentsen–Rio Grande Valley State Park, each day began with the raucous cries of golden-fronted woodpeckers, green jays,

Our Life with Birds

and plain chachalacas. One of the delights of camping is awakening to the dawn chorus of the birds. This, however, was a dawn cacophony. "Look at me! Look at me!" each bird seemed to be screaming. "It's mine! It's mine!"

High overhead in a Texas ebony tree, the white-winged doves were cooing and carrying on. Puffing out his chest, a male would sail out from the tree and glide in a circle on set wings, white patches flashing in the orange rays of the rising sun. Returning to the tree near his prospective mate, he would then bob up and down, cooing as loudly as possible. "Don't I look fine?"

Great-tailed grackles paraded through the campground, the males with beaks pointed skyward and tails folded to V-shaped keels, their raucous, rusty-gate voices crying for attention. And, on the ground nearby, a bronzed cowbird strutted around a female that seemed to regard his advances with dour skepticism. Then, with every feather ruffled until he looked like an iridescent black tennis ball, he rose straight into the air and hovered three feet above her for nearly a minute before dropping exhausted to the ground.

More suave and sophisticated, a groove-billed ani approached his lady with a gift. Sidling up to her as she sat on an overhanging limb, he proffered a small, thorny branch in his massive, almost puffinlike beak. She accepted it as coyly as if it had been a rose, and the two sat side by side for a moment before flying off together, perhaps to add the branch to a growing nest hidden in a nearby thicket.

Returning northward later in the week, we again stopped at Lake Corpus Christi for the night and claimed our old campsite without thinking of the consequences. With the dawn came a familiar sound, "thump, thump." The cardinal had lost none of his jealous ardor in the intervening days. Ah, what a price we pay for land and love.

A Place to Call Home: 1998

Small groups of American goldfinches swirl around our backyard feeders, sharing the sunflower and thistle seeds that help sustain them through the winter months. At the same time, raucous flocks of common grackles and red-winged blackbirds sweep through the neighborhood, gleaning acorns from the oaks and stalking haughtily across the lawn in search of insects, worms, and seeds.

These birds are highly social during the winter months, but that will change dramatically as they move northward to their breeding grounds in spring. Each pair will then establish a territory in which to nest and raise their young, a territory they will aggressively protect against all others of their species.

By the same token, our resident birds are already proclaiming ownership of selected tracts. A northern mockingbird sings from dawn to dusk and chases everything that ventures near, while a Carolina wren chortles loudly in defense of its backyard domain.

Our recognition of territory "ownership" in birds dates far back into antiquity. Aristotle, in about 350 b.c., wrote, "Each pair of eagles needs a large territory and on that account allows no other eagle to settle in the neighborhood." Zenodotus, a century later, observed that "one bush does not shelter two robins."

It is not merely pride of ownership that fuels this drive. There are numerous physical and psychological advantages to establishing and defending a territory. An isolated male is free to court any female that may enter his domain without interference from other males, and ownership seems to be a powerful stimulus in the reproductive process, the ultimate aphrodisiac.

Isolation also reduces competition during nest building and the raising of the young. Because this isolation means less contact with other members of the species, there is less chance of promiscuity, an important concern when the male assists his mate in chores around the nest.

Equally important is the fact that the establishment of a territory provides a monopoly on nearby food resources. This becomes vital as the pair seeks to provide for their ever-hungry nestlings. As Joel Carl Welty noted, "A robin's worst enemy—his greatest competitor—is not a hawk or cat. It is another robin which seeks from the environment exactly those kinds of food, those nesting sites, and that kind of a mate, that all robins seek."

The mutual antagonism of male birds during the breeding season also leads to dispersal of the species across the landscape. If all were to cluster around selected feeding areas, they would soon strip them of their bounty. Meanwhile, other habitats and their resources would be neglected. Dispersion reduces potential overpopulation and promotes efficient use of the land and the available nesting sites. At the same time, it may serve to reduce the incidence of contagious diseases and to make it more difficult for predators to find the isolated nests.

Carolina wren

Once they have settled into discrete territories, birds also become intimately familiar with the surroundings, learning where to find food and where to seek shelter from inclement weather and potential predators. Escape routes are imprinted in their memories; daily life falls into a peaceful routine.

As evidence of the psychological advantage of ownership, one has only to look at numerous field studies involving competing birds. When an interloper is caged within another's territory, he is quickly attacked and cowers before the resident's aggressive posturing. When the roles are reversed, however, the other quickly becomes the aggressor.

There are many variations on the territorial theme. Some birds demand enormous areas for nesting and feeding, whereas others defend much smaller tracts. Large raptors may require several square miles; a tiny warbler, but a fraction of an acre.

Most of the songbirds defend territories in which they mate, nest, and feed. They then join larger migrating flocks and become more social during the winter months. A few birds, however, establish winter territories as well, chasing away competitors for the limited food reserves.

Birds defend their territories by singing and posturing, by pursuing intruders, and, less frequently, by actually fighting. Usually the males arrive on the breeding grounds first and establish their claims, singing from exposed perches to proclaim ownership of their chosen tracts. They then wait for the females to arrive, and the females' choice of mates may be dictated as much by the quality of the territories as by the beauty or voice of the courting males.

So strong is the attraction to a favored territory that many birds return to the same place to nest year after year, particularly if previous efforts were successful. Indeed, this site fidelity is probably the bond that keeps many pairs together.

Each avian species has its own idea of what constitutes the perfect home. Some, such as purple martins, gulls and terns, and several of the herons and other large wading birds, choose crowded tenements and fly far afield in search of food for their young. Others, such as the robin or mockingbird, prefer to nest in solitude and forage close to home.

For each, there is an innate urge to "own" a plot of land, however large or small, an area claimed by song and defended if necessary with determined skirmishes. An individual bird's success, and the future of its genes, may well depend on the quality of its chosen territory.

Birds as Builders: 1996

There has been a dramatic surge in home building throughout our neighborhood in recent weeks. Several families have moved into an apartment complex down the street, and others have set up housekeeping on the surrounding lots. These developments will not show up in the government's latest economic statistics, but they are vital to the success of the avian community. Most of our resident birds are now absorbed in building nests and raising young.

The daily lives of even our most common birds provide interesting contrasts. Each builds a nest characteristic of its species, and each employs unique methods to assure the survival of its eggs and newly hatched young.

Thus, purple martins swirl around a high-rise apartment, while a pair of mockingbirds build their nest deep in the sheltering confines of a yaupon thicket. Not far away, a mourning dove incubates its two white eggs on a flimsy platform of twigs saddled on the exposed limb of a cedar elm. The poor craftsmanship of the dove would likely embarrass the more skillful mockingbird, and both of these solitary species shun the social whirl of the gregarious and garrulous martins.

Thousands of royal and Sandwich terns nest in compact colonies on islands in Galveston Bay, each sitting just out of pecking range of its nearest neighbors. They share the limited sand beaches and shell reefs available to them and then forage far out over the open water. Studies show that the oldest and most experienced terns occupy the center of the colony, where they undoubtedly derive protection from prowling predators. Nests on the fringes are more likely to be robbed, but enough eggs will survive to assure perpetuation of the species.

Our large wading birds, too, are colonial nesters, sharing close quarters even with other species. Herons, egrets, ibises, and spoonbills often crowd together in the waterfront trees and bushes, where intruders are faced by a mob of irate, sharp-billed, screaming defenders.

Some birds build their nests high in the treetops, out of reach of many terrestrial predators. Others rely on stealth and camouflage, concealing their homes in dense foliage or amid sheltering grasses or reeds.

Nests of North American birds range in size from the tiny cups of the hummingbirds to the giant penthouse of the bald eagle. The former, built of delicate plant down and spiderwebs, and perhaps camouflaged with lichens, may be scarcely larger than a golf ball and resemble a knot on a tree limb. The eagle's nest, on the other hand, is used year after year by the same pair and gradually grows to enormous proportions. Some may be more than ten feet high and weigh nearly a ton. At times, host trees have collapsed under the weight of such massive nests.

Asked to describe a "typical" bird nest, we might choose the carefully crafted home of the American robin, a sturdy cup of mud and grasses lined with soft, comfortable plant fibers. However, the variations seem limitless. Sticks, smaller twigs, weed stems, grasses, leaves, Spanish-moss, feathers, and a host of discarded human products are used as nest-building materials. Some birds take several days in their painstaking preparations; others simply pull together a pile of debris and move right in.

The goldfinches that spend the winter in our backyard move northward to breed, normally late in the spring when the thistles have gone to seed. Their carefully woven nests are lined with thistledown and are so compact that they may fill with water if not protected from the elements by the incubating or brooding parents.

Song sparrows were once known in the country as "horsehair birds" because of their penchant for lining their nests with the hairs from horses' tails. Deprived of that resource, they turn to other materials, and we found one such nest lined completely with slender red stalks from the spore capsules of sphagnum moss.

Great crested flycatchers often ornament their nests with castoff snakeskins, whereas tree swallows incorporate soft, white feathers. And during several days in a photo blind at the Anahuac National Wildlife Refuge, we once watched a nesting coot bring fresh water-lily flowers to its nest each morning.

The cliff swallow rolls small balls of mud and carries them in its beak, meticulously constructing a solid, juglike nest with the opening on the side. Modern highway bridges and culverts provide suitable shelter for this charming swallow, allowing it to expand its range across the state from its original rocky cliffs.

In contrast to the cliff swallow's covered mud nest, the barn swallow's nest is an open cup of mud and grasses. Bank swallows dig burrows into the vertical walls of old gravel pits or road cuts, while tree swallows prefer abandoned woodpecker holes or other tree cavities.

Our Life with Birds

With their sturdy beaks and heavily ossified skulls, the woodpeckers are well suited for excavating nest holes in even the hardest wood, thereby deriving a degree of protection for their broods. Other birds then make use of these custom-built homes, and abandoned woodpecker holes may house such varied species as chickadees, bluebirds, screech-owls, and wood ducks.

An oriole's intricately woven, pendant nest or the large, painstakingly hewn cavity of a pileated woodpecker requires an enormous investment in time and effort, and not all birds go to such extremes. The ubiquitous killdeer simply lays its eggs right on the ground, as does the common nighthawk. Each might choose a scenic site on a sandy beach, the shoulder of a gravel road, or even the flat roof of a suburban shopping center.

Nesting strategies and avian architecture vary enormously, and each instinctive technique profoundly affects the types of eggs birds lay, dictating the color, size, and shape those eggs will take. They are as uniquely formed and patterned as the birds that lay them.

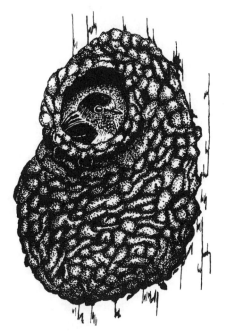

Cliff swallow nest

A Nest Full of Eggs: 1996

The American robin incubates its four sky blue eggs in the safety of a sturdy, cuplike nest built of mud and grasses. Perched high on a tree limb, the nest offers protection for the tiny young that hatch from the eggs blind and naked. It will be at least two weeks before the fledglings are mature enough to leave the security of that nest.

Nearby, on a patch of bare ground, a killdeer tends its four buff-colored eggs that are mottled and blotched with camouflage colors. Baby killdeer, however, emerge from their eggs covered with downy feathers and with their eyes open. As soon as they dry out and regain their strength, they are able to scamper about and hide from marauding predators.

Although the adult robin and killdeer have about the same body size, the female killdeer lays an egg almost twice as large as that of the robin. Incubation requires twenty-four to twenty-eight days for the larger killdeer egg, but only twelve to fourteen days for the robin egg.

In other words, the baby robin hatches quickly in the smaller egg and develops further in the shelter of the nest. The helpless hatchling is known as an "altricial" baby. The "precocial" killdeer, on the other hand, develops more fully within the larger egg and derives protection from its camouflage plumage and early mobility when it finally hatches. Other precocial young include the familiar ducks and barnyard chickens.

Owls, woodpeckers, kingfishers, and other birds that nest in tree cavities or in burrows normally lay white eggs. There is no need for camouflage patterns or colors with this concealment, and the metabolic resources needed for a final "paint job" can be channeled to other uses.

Eggs laid in open nests, however, require more protection from predators that might spot them unattended. Hence, most are colored in shades of pale blue, green, or brown, often spotted and blotched with darker hues. The camouflage reaches its ultimate development in the ground-nesting birds such as sandpipers, plovers, gulls, and terns. Their eggs so closely match the sand, gravel,

Killdeer chick and eggs

or other substrate on which they rest that they are almost invisible, even at close range.

There may even be a degree of variability within a single species. Colonial royal and Sandwich terns, for example, lay eggs that range from white or buff to pale pink, with complex patterns of brown or black. These variations probably help the adult tern locate her own egg as she returns to the colony where hundreds of eggs dot the ground.

We often use the term "egg shaped" to mean pyriform, with one end smaller than the other. Not all bird eggs, however, have this stereotypical form. Owl eggs are almost perfectly round. With the clutch deposited securely in a nest cavity, there is nowhere for the eggs to roll, and there apparently has been no driving force to develop a more stable shape.

Murres, on the other hand, lay uniquely elongated eggs that are sharply pointed at one end. These seabirds nest on oceanside cliffs, the eggs deposited directly on the bare rock of narrow, perilous ledges. Laying rounded eggs would invite certain disaster, but the long, pointed murre eggs spin around in a circle if nudged and do not even roll.

Doves, pigeons, and nighthawks lay eggs with both ends rounded, and the fast-flying hummingbirds, swifts, and swallows also have relatively long, elliptical eggs. These shapes are dictated by the pelvic bones in the birds' streamlined bodies.

Some birds lay but a single egg, whereas others lay several in each clutch. Depending on the length of the breeding season, some may also raise two or more broods a year; others renest only if the first clutch is destroyed.

The royal terns that breed on islands in Galveston Bay normally lay only one egg, but the tiny least terns lay two. Most hummingbirds also lay two eggs. The average clutch size of the laughing gull is three, although nests may hold from two to four. Sandpipers and plovers almost invariably lay four markedly pyriform eggs, and the incubating birds carefully turn them so that they all point inward, like the leaflets of a four-leaf clover or the slices of a pie, thereby providing a compact clutch they can cover with their bodies. Because the precocial shorebirds have very large eggs for their body size, it is unlikely they could successfully hatch more than four.

These species are called "determinate layers," producing a fixed number of eggs and no more in a single nesting. Others are "indeterminate layers," birds that apparently produce additional eggs until the clutch feels right. Ducks and chickens are examples of indeterminate layers, and some of our wild duck species fill their nests with a dozen eggs or more. If some are removed, the female may continue to lay.

The record chicken produced 364 eggs in one year, but not all prolific egg producers are gallinaceous birds or waterfowl. A northern flicker laid a phenomenal 71 eggs in seventy-three days when researchers removed them from the nest, leaving but a single "nest egg" to provide incentive.

Variations in the color, shape, and number of bird eggs abound. Within a particular species, birds nesting farther north normally have larger clutches, presumably because they can feed their young through more daylight hours. The increased productivity also compensates for the hazards of long migration flights.

Other species, including the northern owls, have larger clutches when food is plentiful. In lean years, females lay fewer eggs, portioning out scarce resources to fewer hungry mouths, thereby ensuring the survival of at least one or two chicks.

At first glance, avian reproduction seems a simple matter: birds

Our Life with Birds

build nests, lay eggs, and raise their young. Closer examination, however, reveals endless permutations and combinations as birds struggle for survival in an amazingly complex environment.

Brood Parasites: 1986

It is spring again, a time of year when, to paraphrase Tennyson, a young bird's fancy lightly turns to thoughts of love. A Carolina wren is singing loudly from the back fence, and the resident chickadees and titmice are busily engaged in less strident courtship. Soon dozens of migrant species will return from tropical America to begin building their nests.

We have seen that birds have a wide variety of nesting habits. Some construct stick platforms or cups of grass high in the tops of trees; others satisfy their primal instincts with simple scrapes on bare ground. Most curious of all, perhaps, are those that have escaped from household chores completely, taking no part in building a nest, incubating their eggs, or rearing their young. These tedious tasks they impose on other birds, usually of another species. The profligate birds, often considered lazy by those who tend to anthropomorphize, are called "brood parasites."

Members of five different bird families throughout the world are known to be obligate parasites; they cannot attain reproductive success without a host. There are many other nonobligate parasites, species that occasionally lay their eggs in another nest but normally incubate their own eggs and raise their own young. The latter group includes such North American species as black-billed and yellow-billed cuckoos, greater roadrunner, brown thrasher, European starling, and house sparrow.

Last summer, for example, a northern cardinal nest in McKinney Falls State Park near Austin, Texas, was found to contain four cardinal eggs and two eggs of a yellow-billed cuckoo. According to the published report in *American Birds,* the cuckoo eggs hatched; the cardinal eggs did not. The host cardinals then fed the young cuckoos for a week before the nest was destroyed by a predator.

The duck family contains the largest number of nonobligate parasites, with twenty-one different species being reported as occasionally laying eggs in the nests of others. The redhead and the ruddy duck are the ones most often involved, and both also show a weaker attachment to their own nests and leave their young at an earlier age.

Obligate brood parasites include several genera of cuckoos, African honey guides, a group of weaverbirds, the black-headed duck of South America, and two genera of cowbirds. These varied and wide-ranging birds know no other way of life.

Found virtually across the continent, the brown-headed cowbird is abundant in our local Houston area. Here it parasitizes a number of other resident species. Many of the nests of red-winged blackbirds are found to contain cowbird eggs or young, as are the nests of buntings, orchard orioles, wood thrushes, flycatchers, and others. According to one study, the five species most frequently parasitized by the cowbird in the northeastern states are the red-eyed vireo, American redstart, yellow warbler, chipping sparrow, and song sparrow.

Some host species react to a cowbird egg by accepting it and incubating it with their own; others may abandon the nest completely upon discovery of the alien egg. At least one host, the yellow warbler, sometimes builds a second nest over the first so the eggs are not incubated and then starts another clutch in the second story. Photographs have been published of a seven-story yellow warbler's nest, each of the lower layers containing a cowbird egg.

Problems arise in a parasitized nest because cowbird eggs hatch a day or two earlier than those of the typical host. Thus, the fast-growing cowbirds are larger and stronger than their nest mates, getting most of the food and even crowding the natural young from the nest. Frequently, only the parasites survive.

The system, of course, has existed through the millennia, with cowbirds following great herds of bison across the plains, stopping to lay eggs in convenient nests wherever they found them. Now, however, they are expanding their range with the clearing of the land and the introduction of domestic animals. And now, too, we are forcing our own sense of values on the phenomenon.

There are several species of rare or endangered birds, for example, that are heavily parasitized by cowbirds. That pressure alone has not caused their decline, but it is a contributing factor when considered with habitat destruction and other constraints we are now forcing on wildlife. Several management plans for endangered species call for control of cowbird populations.

The Kirtland's warbler that nests only in a small area in Michigan is being helped in its struggle for survival by trapping and removing brown-headed cowbirds, and the yellow-shouldered blackbird of Puerto Rico benefits from similar control of the island's glossy cowbirds. An extensive cowbird-trapping project in the region around Austin, Texas, allowed production of a number of black-capped vireos where few had successfully hatched in previous years.

Such controls may now be necessary to preserve some of our rarest songbird species; however, the instinctive behavior of brood parasites should not be judged by our own standards of right and wrong. It is simply another of nature's many ways birds solve the problem of procreation.

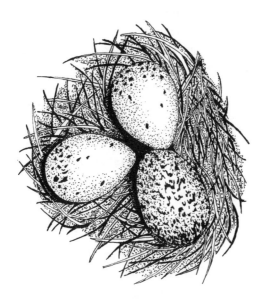

Brown-headed cowbird egg in nest of red-eyed vireo

Much of a bird's life revolves around the substantial task of rearing one or more broods of chicks. There are nests to build, eggs to incubate, and hatchlings to feed. That accomplished, the parents must then teach their young the avian skills necessary to survive in an incredibly complex and hostile world. Within those general guidelines, however, birds employ many different strategies. Even the parental roles of the two sexes vary enormously with the species.

In some cases, both parents share equally in the domestic chores, building the nest and caring for the young together. Either might be found incubating the clutch of eggs, and both bring food to feed the hungry chicks.

Most, however, employ another strategy in which the female does much of the nest building and incubates alone, while the male feeds her at the nest. Both sexes then join in caring for the babies. In such cases, the female is often less colorful than her mate. His job is to claim a territory and protect it against intruders with song and flamboyant displays. Meanwhile, cloaked in drabber camouflage plumage, she sits quietly on the nest.

The male red-winged blackbird takes no part in domestic chores at all. His sole duty is to protect his domain and mate with a harem of females that build their own nests, incubate their eggs, and raise their young alone. In keeping with these roles, the familiar male is glossy black with flaring red epaulettes. The smaller female, on the other hand, wears less conspicuous streaked brown garb.

Phalaropes employ a very different reproductive tactic. In a striking role reversal, the male incubates the eggs and cares for the chicks. Once her eggs are laid, the female's job is done, and she wanders off to lead an active social life. In this case, she wears the vivid plumage, while her mate's attire is more subdued. It is the male phalarope, too, that acquires a brood patch during the nesting season.

Incubation requires the transfer of heat from the brooding bird to the eggs. Because feathers are poor thermal conductors, birds develop areas of bare skin, called brood patches, on the belly to make contact with the eggs. Stimulated by hormonal flow, the feathers are lost shortly before the clutch is complete, and the skin becomes spongy and inflamed with enlarged blood vessels.

In general, brood patches occur only in the sex that incubates. If both share in the task, both usually have such brood patches; however, a number of male songbirds lack the patches and merely cover the eggs to slow heat loss when the female is absent.

Ducks and geese create a type of brood patch by plucking downy feathers from their breasts and using them to line the nest; penguins and murres warm the eggs by holding them on top of their feet. Each is effective in its own way.

Birds that nest in the hot Texas sun often have quite another problem, particularly if they lay their eggs directly on the ground. Too much heat can be as deadly as the cold, and some species engage in what is known as "belly soaking" to cool the clutch. A tern nesting on a sandy beach or a killdeer sheltering its eggs on a patch of gravel may walk into the water and wet its belly feathers thoroughly. It then fluffs its feathers and settles back down on the nest, cooling the moistened eggs by evaporation.

Some species wait until the clutch is complete before beginning incubation. Because the eggs do not begin to develop until warmed, this delayed incubation assures that the young will hatch synchronously. It is best, for example, that baby ducklings hatch at the same time so they can troop together after their mother as she leads them to the water.

If a bird begins incubating when the first egg is laid, the babies will hatch sequentially over a period of several days. Owls employ this strategy, and the stair-step siblings differ greatly in size and vigor. In periods of plenty, all may survive, but if food is scarce, it will all go to the largest and strongest. Although this may seem harsh, it assures the survival of at least a portion of the brood.

Feeding its hungry young becomes a full-time job for every avian parent. Terns and gulls along our coast feed their chicks on small fish and other marine life, while doves and pigeons provide secretions called "pigeon milk" from the lining of their crops. Some of the larger hawks specialize in rodents, while others are primarily

Wilson's phalarope

bird hunters. Herons bring to the nest a tantalizing soup of partially digested fish, frogs, small reptiles, amphibians, snails, and other tasty morsels, which they regurgitate into the probing beaks of their insatiable babies. Most songbirds feed insects to their young, even if they are primarily seedeaters as adults. The insects provide a richer protein source that assures rapid growth, a priority in raising any baby bird.

Altricial babies are fed in the nest, but precocial young leave the nest site shortly after hatching to follow their parents, receiving food as they scurry along and learning to forage for themselves.

There is little time to learn these skills, for many of the fledglings must be ready to migrate when autumn comes. Even though still in immature plumage, the young birds take to the air, making what seems an impossible journey.

Some join large flocks in preparation for the migration flight. Purple martins, for example, assemble for several weeks in enormous roosts before striking out for the tropics, while geese congregate and fly in compact skeins. Whooping cranes travel in family groups, each chick accompanying its parents to the Texas coast in the fall and back to Canada the following spring, eventually establishing its own territory nearby. Its parental education lasts for many months.

Some adult shorebirds, on the other hand, depart their Arctic breeding grounds first, perhaps to spend the winter in South America. The young follow later, finding their own way alone to a land they have never seen, navigating by a mysterious map etched in their genes.

Our Life with Birds

There are as many reproductive strategies and parental roles as there are bird species. Each has evolved in response to particular conditions, and each is successful in its own way.

Minding the Kids: 1998

It is a cool fifty-degree morning in early June as we launch a canoe from the sandy beach and paddle slowly along the shore of Leech Lake's Kabekona Bay. This is a wonderful time to visit Minnesota's great North Woods, and we never tire of exploring the forest trails and winding waterways. Our cabin at Bailey's Resort is quiet and secluded, and owners Doug and Carol Pitt go out of their way to make our annual visit a rewarding one. *(Dana and Cindy Pitt now own and operate the resort.)*

A few fluffy clouds frame the rising sun, and strong winds of the previous day have given way overnight to a gentle breeze. We glide effortlessly through yellow water-lilies in full bloom and watch as the sky brightens and the water reflects the white-trunked birches and towering Norway pines along the shore.

A female common goldeneye and her brood swim nearby. The newly hatched ducklings, just out of their nest box beside the harbor, paddle furiously to dive beneath the surface, only to pop quickly up again like fuzzy little tennis balls. With their dark, downy plumage and white cheek patches, they are our favorites among the many ducklings we encounter on our daily rounds.

The goldeneyes seem amazingly independent, even at so early an age, often swimming off by themselves to investigate sheltered nooks along the bank. As we approach, however, the hen gives a sharp alarm call, and the ducklings rush to fall in behind her, paddling so fast that they rise to run across the water.

A hen mallard, too, has her brood in tow, eight half-grown ducklings that hang close to her flanks. The goldeneyes seem immediately curious and adventuresome, but the mallards seldom venture far from their mother. They are unconcerned by our presence, however, and swim on ahead of us, staying just off the bow of our canoe.

Entering the mouth of the Kabekona River, we wind upstream through dense beds of wild rice and water-lilies. Behind these aquatic plants lie broad fringes of sedge marsh where black terns swirl gracefully on long, slender wings and yellow-headed blackbirds squabble over territories in a patch of cattails.

Mink frogs call from the edges of the marsh, like strumming loose strings on a guitar. Brightly colored dragonflies hover on transparent wings, dipping occasionally to lay eggs in the tannin-stained water of the river.

Approaching a patch of sedges that has torn loose upstream and forms a small floating island along the bank, we slow our pace and drift noiselessly closer on the breeze, finally coming to a stop among the water-lilies. There on the island, neck stretched low and bill almost touching the water, sits a loon on its nest of sodden sedges. Male or female, we cannot tell, for both sexes share in the incubation of the two olive brown eggs, and their plumages are virtually identical.

Once the eggs hatch, the pair will take their precocial chicks out on the open water of the lake. Tucked safely beneath a protecting wing, the tiny balls of gray down will frequently ride along on their parents' backs.

We have paddled past this nest each day on our forays up the river, and we know that its occupant has come to accept us and will tolerate our presence. Staying well away, we ready a telephoto lens and photograph this lovely scene.

The state bird of Minnesota, the common loon is resplendent in white-flecked black plumage. Its dark head is glossed with green; its red eyes gleam brightly above a dagger bill. Absolutely motionless, it stares back at these silent intruders floating quietly among the lily pads. For several minutes, we simply sit and enjoy this signature tableau, one of which we never tire. Then, slowly and carefully, we dip our paddles and slide away, thrilled with yet another intimate encounter with the bird that embodies the spirit of the North.

On upstream, we surprise a blue-winged teal with her young. Immediately, the ducklings hide among the sedges, while the hen flaps noisily away across the surface, trying desperately to decoy us

Baby common goldeneye

with her "broken wing." How different her behavior, we reflect, than that of the placid mallard with her brood.

A male red-winged blackbird perches atop a cattail and loudly sings his strident songs, his harem of females arrayed around him, each on her own nest. Most are well hidden among the reeds, but we discover one female on a nest along the water's edge, and she flies up at our approach. Pausing for a moment and peeking into the carefully woven pouch, we find four pale blue green eggs beautifully scrawled with brown and black. Then we quickly turn and paddle away, as both male and female berate us loudly for our intrusion.

Passing under a roadway bridge, we watch scores of cliff swallows peering out of their mud-jug nests on the girders above the water. Such artificial "cliffs" have allowed these graceful birds to expand their range across the country, nesting under virtually every bridge and overpass throughout the region.

Then, from the sedges beside us, comes a furious uproar. A female wood duck runs squealing across the water, both wings flailing, spray flying in all directions. We look back quickly and spot a half-dozen downy ducklings just vanishing into a little channel in the marsh. For a hundred yards, the hen leads us on, then abruptly jumps into flight and circles back, her shrill cries signaling her approach to her hidden brood.

The marshes and surrounding forests are filled with birds at this season of the year, and each has unique instincts for successfully raising and protecting its young. We feel privileged to share in this avian pageant staged on a lovely June morning on one of Minnesota's more scenic waterways.

7

Migration: The Frequent Fliers

Many of our birds make long-distance, round-trip migration flights every year, heading south from the United States and Canada to Central or South America in the fall and returning again in spring to build their nests and rear their young. Species in numerous avian families, ranging from large hawks to tiny hummingbirds, compose this vast array of Neotropical migrants, all moving to warmer climates during our winter season to assure an ample supply of food. Other species, meanwhile, migrate shorter distances, perhaps from the northern tier of states to the Deep South. All follow instinctive urges and prescribed routes etched in their genes, selecting the migratory behavior that offers them the highest potential for survival.

The Long and Short of It: 1996

The last week in April marks the peak of the spring bird migration in much of Texas. Hordes of colorful warblers, buntings, tanagers, and orioles swarm across our coast on their return from tropical America, many of them flying nonstop across the Gulf of Mexico from launching points on the Yucatán Peninsula.

The feats of some of these Neotropical migrants are phenomenal. The tiny blackpoll warbler flies from its breeding grounds in the boreal forests of Canada and Alaska all the way to central South

America in the fall and retraces that route in spring. It makes one of the longest flights of any songbird.

The upland sandpiper migrates between the U.S. Great Plains and the pampas of Argentina, while the Arctic tern divides its time between the Arctic and Antarctic regions, flying nearly around the world each year to enjoy the rewards of summer in both hemispheres. Yet, in spite of the monumental distances involved, each returns unerringly to its own ancestral nesting grounds in spring.

Not all birds are long-distance migrants, however. Nor are birds the only animals that travel systematically with the seasons. Our wildlife adopts a wide spectrum of seasonal strategies, each suited to an individual's specific needs.

Many of the colorful warblers spend the winter in the tropics, where they are assured an abundant supply of the insects on which they feed. Although they might survive the cold temperatures of a northern winter, they would quickly starve as rations became impossible to find.

The yellow-rumped warbler, however, supplements its insect diet with wax-myrtle berries and other small fruits, a trait that accounts for the common name of the eastern race, "myrtle warbler." This feeding habit also allows the species to remain throughout the winter in the Houston area.

Blackpoll warbler

Birds that feed mainly on seeds can endure colder climates than can birds that rely on ephemeral insects. Many of the seed-eating finches wander to the southern states in winter only when cone crops fail in the evergreen forests of the far North. In the same manner, several species of northern owls move southward when cyclic rodent populations crash.

Loons, grebes, cormorants, and other diving birds desert their freezing domains for open water along southern shorelines or in warmer lakes. Turkey vultures stream southward in fall from across the United States, seeking warmer weather that creates the towering thermals on which they sail in search of food. All of these migrant species are now en route to their breeding territories, some to remain in Texas, some to venture even beyond the Arctic Circle.

Not all birds of a single species share the same migrational strategies. Recent studies have shown that two-thirds of female song sparrows move southward to more benign climates in winter, yet only one-half of the males choose to migrate. Presumably, males remain closer to the choice territories they will defend in spring, thereby gaining an advantage over their competitors.

Birds of the high mountains may follow an entirely different kind of migration strategy. Instead of heading south for the winter, they merely descend to lower elevations, returning again in spring to the windswept heights. They make what has been called a "vertical migration," or "altitudinal migration," rather than a latitudinal one. The distance in miles may be relatively small, but the benefits can be enormous.

Brown-capped rosy-finches, for example, nest above timberline on the tundra of tall Colorado peaks. In winter, they move down into the valleys, even invading backyard feeders in bustling cities and towns. This, too, is bird migration, although in quite a different form than that of the blackburnian warbler, which is now returning from the rain forests of Venezuela to find a nesting site in the woodlands of the northern states or Canada.

If it seems impossible that small and seemingly fragile birds can make such long and hazardous journeys, consider the migrations of butterflies. The familiar monarch fans out across the continent in summer, spawning several broods that reach beyond the Canadian border. In the fall, however, the last adults wing their way southward once again, funneling down through Texas to spend the winter in a mountain forest in Mexico that they have never seen.

Other butterflies, too, move northward each spring and summer from population reservoirs that survive the winter in the Deep South, producing progeny as they go. Many will be lost with the first freeze of autumn, but others move southward again as the days grow shorter.

Less predictable are mass dispersals in the face of overpopulation. Butterfly populations sometimes reach epic proportions, particularly after plentiful rains contribute to rapid growth of larval food plants. Emerging adult butterflies then stage enormous flights, sometimes over large distances, to find new habitats.

Even mammals migrate when their lifestyles make such programmed journeys necessary. Huge numbers of Brazilian free-tailed bats inhabit caves in the Texas Hill Country, emerging each summer night to feed on the insects that fuel their flights. In the fall, as insect populations drop, the bats head southward in the manner of the migrant birds, returning to their caves again in spring.

Giant gray whales migrate southward along the Pacific Coast from the seas surrounding Alaska to the warm, shallow bays of Baja California. There they give birth to their young and return northward only when the lengthening days promise an end to icebound seas.

Humans, too, share many of these strategies employed by wildlife, spending the winter months in the South and returning home to cooler climates as spring approaches. Birds, bats, and butterflies, however, find their way without benefit of road signs or maps, making wildlife migration one of the true wonders of the natural world.

Birds of a Feather: 1988

We wake in the night and lie quietly listening, not quite sure what has disturbed our sleep. It is a wet, foggy winter night, and the streetlight outside our window casts a yellow glow through the low-hanging mist. Then we hear it again, the nasal, resonant cries of snow geese. It is a wonderfully wild sound, and we smile at each other in delight. The querulous avian conversations continue for several minutes as the long skeins pass low overhead. Then, all too soon, the music fades in the distance, and we hear only the drip of moisture from the trees.

The great flocks of geese that descend on the prairies and rice fields of coastal Texas in winter provide one of the real treats of the season, not only for eager waterfowl hunters but for all who appreciate our wildlife. It is a special thrill to see thousands of the large birds rise as one from a field or to watch the long, ragged formations passing overhead against the wind.

Other birds, too, have now formed large aggregations. Rafts of ducks can be found floating on our bays and lakes, and concentrations of shorebirds poke and patter about on the beaches and in the marshes. Enormous flocks of grackles and blackbirds feed in the fields and roost together in the trees at night, moving from place to place in swirling columns like smoke from prairie fires.

White- and blue-morph snow geese

We are all familiar with the tendency of these birds to assemble in flocks, but surprisingly little is known about the dynamics of such groups. It seems impossible, for example, that they can twist and turn in flight in such near-perfect synchronization. Each individual seems almost to be aware of the intentions of the others or to react instantaneously to their movements.

Very few birds lead solitary lives outside the breeding season, but most do not unite in permanent year-round flocks. The normal sequence for many species is to pair up and seek secluded nesting territories, then to form flocks again as the young become more mobile. There are several reasons for the flocking instinct and many benefits to flock members.

The geese may benefit in their long migrations and daily flights by sharing the tasks of navigation and of leading the flock. Older, more experienced birds would seemingly know the route, while younger ones follow close behind. A constant changing of the lead position distributes the tiring burden of bucking the wind.

Foraging flocks are presumably more efficient in finding food. One individual might spot a rich cache that the others would have missed. Together they move through an area and sweep it clean.

Birds of several species have also been discovered roosting together in groups in order to keep warm. Creepers, kinglets, or bluebirds may join others of their species in a tree hollow or sheltered nook to sleep through the night in a feather ball. One European ornithologist discovered more than sixty wrens crowding each night into a nest box less than six inches square. Our little Inca doves, too, have been observed in cold weather roosting in layers two or three birds deep. In one experiment on the energetics of communal roosting, it was determined that four starlings huddled together in near-freezing temperatures conserved enough heat to lower their metabolic rates by 48 percent.

Whether flocks are migrating, feeding, or simply keeping warm, there are always added benefits in increased protection from predators. A flock has many eyes and ears; an individual, but two.

Both physical advantages and the instinctive social urge common to most animals may play a part in flocking behavior. Whatever the driving force, the result is that winter bird flocks and migrating hordes provide a wonderful wildlife spectacle.

George Whetstone noted in his *Promos and Cassandra* in 1578: "Byrds of a fether, best flye together." And, in more modern form, Robert Burton wrote in *The Anatomy of Melancholy* in the seventeenth century, "Birds of a feather will gather together." Actually, the phrase originated with neither of these authors, for it is a proverb found in virtually every language from the beginning of the written record.

We accept the fact that outside the literary world as well, birds of the same species tend to congregate. We expect to see skeins of geese flying overhead or flocks of robins or red-winged blackbirds poking about the backyard or swirling over the fields. Yet there are also frequent examples of mixed flocks, where birds of different species band together, apparently having never read the classical literature.

In most cases, they are closely related birds with similar feeding habits. Several species of ducks might swim in the same small pond, for example, or a large winter blackbird flock might contain red-wings, grackles, and cowbirds. Sometimes they mix freely; sometimes they form discrete species groups within the larger flock.

So, too, do migrating flocks of small passerines that stream through the night sky, headed southward from their breeding grounds in North America in autumn or returning from the tropics with the spring. The discriminating ear can detect chip notes of many different species as they pass overhead or as they descend together into the trees to rest and feed.

Very different, however, are the mixed flocks of small songbirds that flood Southeast Texas during the winter months. Warblers, vireos, chickadees, titmice, creepers, kinglets, and gnatcatchers may all band together in a loosely knit feeding flock and go trooping together through the trees, picking and poking into every curled leaf and under every loose slab of bark.

One might expect birds to be uniformly distributed through the

Carolina chickadee

winter woodlands, each seeking its own private insect food supply. Such is not the case. Instead, large areas may be virtually empty of birds. Then a feeding flock arrives, and there is a brief flurry of activity, with dozens of feathered mites flitting about, chattering amiably among themselves. Soon they are gone again, and the only movement is that of a leaf swirling slowly down.

This would seem at first poor use of limited food resources, but quite the opposite is true. If each bird were to forage on its own, it might spend much of its time covering territory another had already investigated. In human terms, it might be convenient to think of feeding flocks as organized search parties, systematically combing the woods for hidden insects.

The food may be apportioned by different preferences and by slightly different feeding habits. The chickadees and titmice will eat seeds as well as insects, while the kinglets and gnatcatchers concentrate only on the latter. Vireos methodically glean insects from the leaves; creepers work on the trunks of the trees. When the flock moves on, not a niche has been left untouched.

Birders seek out these feeding flocks and examine them carefully for unusual species. If a summer warbler has lingered too long before heading south, or if a migrant has wandered far off course, it will probably cast its lot with such a group.

Even in our backyard, the birds come and go in these feeding flocks. We will hear the call of a chickadee and look out to see several birds of a half-dozen species swarming through the willow oaks and cedar elms. Then, just as quickly, they are gone, but their visit has provided one of the day's delights.

What Drives Them On?: 1985/1997

Of all the bird species that breed in North America, nearly a quarter are Neotropical migrants. They spend a considerable portion of their lives in tropical America, where the insects, fruits, and flowers on which they feed are present in abundance during our more spartan winter season.

These migrants know no taxonomic bounds. They include the flycatchers, swallows, thrushes, vireos, tanagers, buntings, orioles, and grosbeaks. Most of the colorful warblers head southward in the fall, as do the hummingbirds and some of our larger hawks. Shorebirds may vacate the windswept Canadian or Alaskan tundra in favor of the South American coastline or the grassy pampas of Argentina, and some of the terns, herons, and gallinules seek similar environments.

Birders exploring exotic tropical locals during the months of our northern winter encounter many familiar birds. Among white-tipped quetzals and handsome fruiteaters in Venezuela's Henri Pittier National Park, we once discovered a Canada warbler. Blackburnian and blackpoll warblers shared the Andean slopes with rose-headed parakeets and collared Incas.

In Trinidad we found, amid white-headed marsh-tyrants, enormous flocks of dickcissels that nest throughout the eastern states. In the rain forests of Amazonian Peru, we saw eastern kingbirds and eastern wood-pewees sharing the trees with pavonine quetzals and paradise jacamars.

Camping on southern Costa Rica's Osa Peninsula some years ago, we delighted in tody-flycatchers building nests over our jungle hammocks and in bare-throated tiger-herons that perched in the trees beside our camp each evening. Among the most abundant birds, however, were chestnut-sided warblers in their greenish winter plumage.

Similarly, on another trip to Costa Rica, we found many of our common species that would soon return to the temperate zone in spring. Among such spectacular tropical birds as trogons, parrots, and honeycreepers were Tennessee, golden-winged, chestnut-sided, hooded, and Kentucky warblers. Feeding with exotic golden-hooded and palm tanagers were more familiar summer tanagers. Six Baltimore orioles shared a tree with a chestnut-mandibled toucan, one of the archetypical birds of the tropical rain forest.

These migratory birds travel thousands of miles in incredible flights, crossing large bodies of water and navigating instinctively by the stars, magnetic fields, and various other means not yet fully understood. It is hard to imagine how a ruby-throated hummingbird can store enough energy in its tiny body to fly nonstop across the Gulf of Mexico between the Yucatán and our Texas coast.

How these birds migrate is a subject that has long been studied, and much remains to be learned. Why they migrate, however, is an equally fascinating question, and one that is frequently ignored.

It is easy to assert, as we did in the first paragraph, that birds withdraw from the northern portions of their range in search of more abundant food supplies. An insect-eating bird, for example, has little choice when its prey succumbs to ice and snow. It must migrate or perish, and it finds a winter refuge in a tropical region that knows no such inclement weather. There it forages among the resident species, seeking an abundance of food in a year-round land of plenty.

Although it may be obvious why birds move southward for the winter, it is less obvious why they choose to return in the spring, risking another long and perilous journey that frequently exacts a heavy toll. Why do these migrants not remain in the tropics throughout the year? There must be some long-range evolutionary benefit to round-trip migration, other than to provide eager bird-watchers with an incomparable springtime pageant.

The answer lies in the way we think of migrant birds. Because they come to our area to breed, we consider them to be temperate species that merely enjoy a winter sojourn in a warmer land. This has long been the approach of most ornithologists, who have studied them mainly on their nesting grounds. Their ecology while in the tropics has been largely ignored until recently.

The phenomenon of migration might be better understood,

point out authors Adrian Forsyth and Ken Miyata in *Tropical Nature,* if we think of migrants as inherently tropical birds. They move northward in spring not so much to return to their ancestral homes, but to take advantage of the summertime abundance in temperate regions.

The sudden eruption of life that accompanies our spring is essentially a temperate-zone phenomenon. Plants burst into bloom, and insects that have overwintered primarily as eggs or pupae emerge in hordes with the lengthening days. There would seem to be an obvious benefit in moving into this newly provisioned ecosystem.

Tropical forests are not subject to such extreme seasonal changes in climate, nor do they exhibit the "feast-or-famine" fluctuations in insect populations. There are, to be sure, variations and cycles even at the equator, but they are not synchronized to the same extent as at higher latitudes.

Neither do tropical days and nights vary in length with the season. Because most birds hunt their prey in daylight, there is more time available to them in the long days of a northern summer than in the standard twelve-hour period of the equatorial zone. Birds nesting in North America, for example, have been shown to raise larger broods than do related tropical species, presumably because they have more hours in which to feed their young.

Thus, the current trend is to regard many of "our" migrant, temperate-zone birds as tropical species that have adapted by moving northward to take advantage of hospitable summer conditions. The synchronous emergence of insects and flowers, the longer daylight hours, and the presence of fewer predators all serve to counteract the dangers of the long journey and make it profitable on an evolutionary basis.

To some, this may seem largely a matter of semantics. But whether we consider these birds to be temperate species that move south for the winter or tropical species that range northward to breed, one overriding fact is clear. The habitats at both ends of the long migration routes are important to the birds' continued survival, and we can no longer ignore tropical rain forests as factors in the ecology of Neotropical migrants. Those forests we visited in Costa Rica are as vital to "our" Kentucky warblers and summer tanagers as they are to the tropical toucans and trogons.

Although it is tempting to think of the southward movements of migrant birds as tropical vacations, nothing could be farther from the truth. Even when they survive the hazards of the long flights and reach the serene shores of a Caribbean island or a lush rain forest in Central or South America, there are no plush avian suites reserved for their arrival. Here they move into territories already populated by year-round residents, other birds with which they must compete for space and food. Many of those residents have established their own hierarchies, and the newcomers must struggle to fit into new and unfamiliar social systems. Young birds, too, face predators that they have never seen and weather patterns with which they are unfamiliar.

Most of the migrants now move into a land area totaling only one-sixth that of the broad expanse of North America in which they nested the previous summer. Here they must find their niches among an inordinately diverse bird community. In many cases, they are forced to change their habits and alter their foraging methods in order to survive.

American redstarts attempt to set up and defend individual feeding territories, much as they did on their breeding grounds far to the north. Bay-breasted warblers, however, join mixed flocks of the permanent residents, trooping through the treetops with a host of exotic tropical birds in search of insect riches.

Black-and-white and Kentucky warblers, on the other hand, frequently join resident birds that specialize in following swarms of army ants to snap up insects flushed by the advancing hordes. Thus, for a few months of the year, these denizens of East Texas woodlands troop around the understory with antbirds, antshrikes, woodcreepers, and other species that have no northern counterparts.

Tennessee warblers, along with orchard and Baltimore orioles, convert from an insect diet to one based on the nectar of tropical flowers. Insectivorous eastern kingbirds, fiercely territorial and competitive during the summer months, gather in large and social flocks in South America, where they feed on berries and other fruits.

Kentucky warbler

Each Neotropical migrant has environmental preferences. Indigo buntings and common yellowthroats are generalists, occupying a variety of brushy, second-growth habitats and surviving even in developed areas. Worm-eating warblers, however, insist on spending their winter months in dense forest tracts, and they face serious trouble with the depletion of the tropical rain forests.

Male hooded warblers likewise claim heavily forested territories, but less aggressive females and immature birds are relegated to second-growth woodlands. Only as they grow older and more experienced will the young learn to compete for choice locations.

Another habitat specialist on its southward migration is the northern waterthrush, which prefers undisturbed mangrove swamps. That environmental niche, too, is rapidly vanishing with the development of coastal estuaries.

Only recently have ornithologists begun to study the requirements of Neotropical migrants in the southern portions of their range. Even though much is known about the nesting habits of the familiar species we consider "our birds," little has been done to study their lives through the remainder of the year. Clearly, many are declining because of habitat losses at both ends of their long migration routes, and the survival of such avian gems as the hooded warbler and the wood thrush may depend on preservation of environments they use during all seasons of the year.

Spring Spectacular: 1997

Fierce easterly winds buffet our van as we drive along the Louisiana coast, and the dark, ominous storm clouds obscure the afternoon sun. A strong frontal system stretching across Texas is sweeping toward us; the forecast promises a weekend of drenching rain.

Reaching the coastal town of Cameron, we join the crowd assembled for the annual spring meeting of the Louisiana Ornithological Society (LOS). Participants have come from every corner of the state on this last weekend in April, traditionally the peak of the migration season at these latitudes. A few ardent birders have even journeyed from more distant regions of the country to join the eager throng.

The Friday evening program takes place to the accompaniment of repeated lightning bursts that lace the sky and thunderclaps that shake the large hall to its foundations. Pelting rain drums loudly on the roof. The storm continues through the night. Winds howl across the coastal marsh, lashing oak and hackberry mottes, driving the rain and hail in blinding sheets. What, we all wonder with some apprehension, will the morning bring?

We awake to a temporary lull in the inclement weather, and we venture out at dawn to find that the rains and winds have brought a host of other visitors to the Louisiana coast. Colorful tanagers, orioles, grosbeaks, and buntings fill mulberry trees throughout the town; warblers of rainbow hue glean insects from the late-flowering pecans.

With Dave Patton and Judith O'Neale, president and secretary-treasurer of the LOS, we join a caravan of birders to scattered woodlots along the coast. Here the birds are even more abundant. They swarm through the trees and hop across the ground around our feet. Thrushes and catbirds seem to be everywhere; vireos comb the foliage for tasty morsels.

It is evident that a major "fallout" has occurred. Migrating birds that wing their way across the Gulf of Mexico from the Yucatán Peninsula have swept across the Louisiana coastline and immediately sought shelter. Here they will rest and feed, refueling before resuming their northward flight once the weather clears. We cannot remember the last time we have seen more spring migrants. Clearly, the weather we feared through the night has brought us avian treasures beyond belief.

We find scores of wood thrushes, their rich, rusty backs and dark-spotted white breasts gleaming in the morning light. Declining dramatically in numbers, this lovely songbird has become a "poster child" for threatened Neotropical migrants, yet on this day we certainly see more than a hundred.

Yellow-throated vireos outnumber even the common red-eyed vireos with which they feed, flashing their bright colors as they pick caterpillars from the foliage of the oaks.

More than once we hear a phrase we had not thought we would ever hear: "Oh, it's just another scarlet tanager." "Just" another gleaming, fluorescent gem, the rival of any rare, exotic species found in the rain forests around the world.

We wade through the thickets and along woodland trails, ankle deep in water from the overnight rains, listening to a serenade of birdsong, enthralled with the abundance all around.

O'Neale spots a Swainson's warbler walking quietly through the brush, and we all ring around it as it feeds unconcerned. Less colorful than most of its close relatives, it is also one of the rarest and most secretive of the warblers, a lifer for several in our group. With this prize are several northern waterthrushes and ovenbirds, other ground-dwelling warblers that make their living on the forest floor. These species, too, are more abundant on this day than on any other in our memory.

We encounter ovenbirds at almost every turn. They stroll across our path with their comical jerky, bobbing gait, short tails cocked upward, orange-striped crowns clearly visible even in the dim forest light. We usually count ourselves fortunate to see three or four migrating ovenbirds on any given day. Today there are undoubtedly hundreds of these strange, aberrant members of the warbler family that take their name from the domed nests they build.

After a quick lunch, we move westward along the coast from Cameron to visit Peveto Woods Sanctuaries owned by the Baton Rouge Audubon Society. Also known as the Holleyman-Sheely Sanctuary, this oak-hackberry motte beside the beach always offers good birding during spring migration. Today it harbors a breathtaking array of birds.

Rose-breasted and blue grosbeaks, scarlet and summer tanagers, Baltimore and orchard orioles, and indigo and painted buntings draw gasps of delight from the assembled birders. We spot four species of woodland thrushes, while flycatchers of several kinds perch overhead and dart out to snap up insects on the wing.

The warblers, however, occupy center stage. A half-dozen species compete for attention in a single tree. Black-and-white warblers creep up and down the branches, while redstarts flit back and forth, flaring their tails to flash the bright orange patches normally concealed when at rest.

Ovenbird

Our Life with Birds

The names alone reflect an artist's palette of brilliant color: blue-winged, golden-winged, yellow, chestnut-sided, black-throated green, bay-breasted, and cerulean. Hooded and Kentucky warblers parade past, their black face patterns setting off their bright yellow plumage. Brilliant blackburnian and magnolia warblers pose overhead with more somber worm-eating and Tennessee warblers.

Assembling once again in Cameron for the evening dinner and program, the group compiles a checklist for the day. It totals a creditable 225 bird species and 34 different warblers. We did not see them all, of course, but this LOS meeting and its well-timed storm have provided the best day of birding that we can remember.

The deluge of birds following the vicious storm along the Louisiana coast was reminiscent of some we had seen decades earlier, yet this was not the only location inundated with avian treasures on that day. Texas, too, received its share. Houstonian Jim Morgan, an experienced and exacting birder who keeps detailed notes of such events, calls April 26, 1997, "the best day of the decade."

Morgan covered the Houston Audubon Society's High Island Sanctuaries and continued on up the coast to Sabine Woods, Sea Rim State Park, and Texas Point National Wildlife Refuge. On his list of migrant perching birds, which he graciously shared with us, he tallied more than 4,000 individuals. "It was," he says, "the best fallout since April 30, 1988."

Mirroring our observations in Louisiana, Morgan reported an estimated 383 wood thrushes and 645 gray catbirds. He also counted 62 Acadian flycatchers and 37 yellow-billed cuckoos, reflecting the diversity of the avian visitors to our coast.

We found yellow-throated vireos to be the most numerous of the vireos in Cameron; however, Morgan found only 18 individuals of this lovely species as compared to 565 red-eyed vireos. At both locations, the ovenbird ranked among the most abundant of the warblers. Morgan, in fact, counted 438 of these charming ground-dwelling birds in his survey, an astonishing 320 of them in one location, at High Island's Smith Oaks woods. He also found more than 250 hooded warblers.

Wood thrush

Birds seemed to be everywhere on that fateful day. It was not necessary to journey to the traditional coastal "hot spots" to observe an impressive fallout. Russ Pitman Park in Bellaire, on the fringes of Houston, also provided urban birders with many thrills. According to Fred Collins, director of the Nature Discovery Center located in the park, participants in a timely Earth Day observance listed 64 different bird species, including the colorful tanagers, grosbeaks, and buntings.

Collins estimated the park contained as many as 400 Tennessee warblers and 50 black-throated green warblers. Others among the 19 warbler species included cerulean, blackburnian, Nashville, blue-winged, yellow, chestnut-sided, magnolia, blackpoll, prothonotary, worm-eating, Kentucky, and hooded warblers; ovenbird; and the yellow-breasted chat.

Smallest of the visiting migrants were the ruby-throated hummingbirds; among the largest was a swallow-tailed kite that circled several times above the park, giving excited watchers excellent views of its elegant black-and-white plumage and deeply forked tail.

Birds attired in every color of the rainbow filled the trees and shrubbery, gleaning insects from the foliage and flying out to snap up tasty morsels in the air. All were refueling after a tiring flight northward from the tropics, some probably following an inland route through South Texas, many more undoubtedly flying non-stop across the Gulf of Mexico from the Yucatán.

Had the weather continued clear and sunny, few of these birds would have stopped in Cameron, High Island, or Bellaire. Most

Our Life with Birds

would probably have continued on along their routes, cruising easily at an elevation of several hundred feet, dispersing widely before stopping to rest and feed somewhere farther inland.

Many left the Yucatán Peninsula at dusk on Thursday evening, striking out on tiny wings across the Gulf, following an instinctive urge and a mysterious route inherent in their genetic makeup. Nearing the Texas-Louisiana coast the following afternoon, they encountered furious winds and heavy rains. Many undoubtedly perished in the storm-lashed sea. Others streamed across the coastal beaches and dropped exhausted into the first shelter they could find. It was a fallout of enormous proportions along the entire western Gulf.

As wind, rain, and even hail continued through Friday night, the birds remained, pinned down by the swirling storm. By Saturday morning, they filled every sheltered niche, too tired to fly, desperately in need of food. This is why we encountered so many birds in Louisiana and why Collins observed that the birding in Russ Pitman Park was "incredible." It is why Morgan found 400 indigo buntings, 150 scarlet tanagers, and an equal number of rose-breasted grosbeaks along the Texas coast.

Not all storm systems provide such fallouts. Two weeks earlier, on April 12, a strong frontal system surged across the Texas coast during the Brazosport Migration Celebration in Lake Jackson, and birders expected a momentous event. It did not materialize.

Coincidentally, Dr. Sidney Gauthreaux was presenting a program about his landmark radar studies of migrating birds at that same meeting, and he called up the weather radar from Corpus Christi on his laptop computer while onstage. Gauthreaux clearly showed that the birds en route to the Texas coast had veered eastward in the face of strong northwesterly winds and would make landfall along the Gulf east of the Mississippi Delta.

On April 26, however, swirling gale-force winds from the east battered the coast as the storm system moved slowly across Texas from the west. Migrating flocks apparently continued toward our coastline, where they encountered the drenching rain and stopped as soon as they could make landfall.

Dr. Gauthreaux's radar work has increased our knowledge of avian migration enormously, but there still are factors we do not yet understand. On the last weekend of April in 1997, however, weather events combined to provide birders with the most remarkable day many had ever experienced. It was undoubtedly a traumatic, or even fatal, day for the birds themselves, but a memorable one for those who came to see them.

8

Gems of the Bird World

Virtually all of our bird families contain species renowned for their beauty. Some are lavishly ornamented with bold and beautiful colors; others are more cryptically patterned with subtle shades that nonetheless prove pleasing to the eye. Categorically, however, some of the most striking of our avian residents are the small migrant songbirds. Included among these diminutive gems are the tanagers, the American warblers, and the hummingbirds.

The Tropical Tanagers: 1988

Few families of birds are more brilliantly colored than the tanagers, an exclusively New World group composed of some two hundred species. Most are residents of the hot, humid forests of Central and South America, where they ornament the treetops with a myriad of rainbow hues.

Only four species occur regularly in North America north of Mexico, but two of those take part in the massive migration that flows across the Texas coast in spring. One, the summer tanager, fans out across the southern United States, with some individuals remaining in East Texas and the Houston area to nest. The other, the scarlet tanager, continues farther north to breed. In autumn, they reverse their flights, returning to the tropical forests that were undoubtedly their ancestral homes.

The other two common North American family members, the western tanager and the hepatic tanager, reside primarily in the Western states, but wander sparingly across Texas. Two others, the flame-colored tanager and the stripe-headed tanager (*now known as the western spindalis*), occur as rare strays in the desert Southwest and Florida, respectively.

The name "tanager" comes from the Amazon region, where the Tupi Indians called them *tangara*. In fact, that word is still used as the scientific name for one of the several tanager genera.

There are no clear-cut familial characteristics, and taxonomic lines are the subject of great ornithological debate. Several species show similarities to the finches, the wood warblers, or even the honeycreepers, and some authors place those anomalous taxa amid other family groups.

The majority tend to be medium-sized, rather chunky birds with moderately heavy beaks. Sexes have similar plumages in certain species; in others there is a high degree of dimorphism. Many females are attired in somber shades of green or brown, the better to remain hidden on the nest. The males, however, are more often colorful. Oh, how very colorful!

The aptly named paradise tanager of South America, for example, sports an incredible combination of turquoise breast shading to purple on the throat; black back, tail, and wings, the latter with a broad blue bar; red and yellow lower back; and a shocking apple green face.

The names of other tropical tanagers are equally descriptive of exotic plumages: glistening-green, beryl-spangled, opal-rumped and opal-crowned, multicolored, green-and-gold and black-and-gold, golden-hooded and golden-crowned, flame-faced, scarlet-bellied, and purple-mantled.

Never will we forget our first look at several tanagers clustered in a low palm tree beside our hotel at Iguaçu Falls in Brazil. From below, they flashed brilliant blue breasts with black throats. Then, as they pirouetted in an avian courtship dance, we could see purple wing patches, orange backs, and iridescent green heads. Paging frantically through the book, we came to an unmistakable likeness; we were looking at green-headed tanagers. *Saira arco iris,* the Argentine authors of the field guide called the birds in Spanish, "rainbow tanagers."

Similarly, we recall a trip to Costa Rica last year, when we struggled to identify a bird seen through the foliage directly overhead. "Bright yellow marked with black, and with a white throat," was the report of some in our group. "Oh no," cried others. "It's black and blue above. And rusty below. There are green flecks all over the head and breast." We were, of course, watching two different birds, an embarrassment of riches. The two feathered gems were our first silver-throated and spangle-cheeked tanagers.

As brilliant as some of these tropical species may be, they hold no exclusive claim to flamboyant fashions. The male scarlet tanager that visits our backyard in Texas is a shocking, almost fluorescent red, set off by jet black wings and tail. So vibrant is his plumage that it seems illuminated by an internal power source; the color glows too brightly to be the product of reflected light.

The female scarlet tanager, on the other hand, is a more subdued yellowish below and olive above, but she possesses a delicate beauty all her own. The other female northern tanagers are similarly attired.

Green-headed tanager

The male summer tanager is a rich, rosy red, like a bright northern cardinal without the crest or black face patch. The hepatic tanager of southwestern mountain forests looks much the same, but with a darker face and bill and plumage marked by a duller shade of red. Even more colorful is the male western tanager, his black wings, tail, and upper back set off against a bright yellow body and flame red head.

Because they feed on insects and berries, our northern tanagers must normally retreat in winter to the warmer environment of tropical America. Each year, however, they return again in spring to brighten our days. There are few birds better at that task.

Avian Butterflies: 1988

Warblers rank at or near the top in popularity with ardent birders and casual watchers alike. These active, charming little creatures swarm through coastal Texas during spring migration, and some remain through the summer months to nest. Arrayed in bright and colorful plumages, they have been called the "butterflies of the bird world" by the great author and artist Roger Tory Peterson.

Charles Maynard wrote nearly ninety years ago: "American Warblers. . . exclusively our own. . . throughout the world we find no finer group of birds, thus they may well be considered the pride of the American ornithologist."

Actually, they are more properly called the wood warblers. Early American naturalists, most of whom came from Europe, mistook these little birds for their familiar Old World warblers, according to Hal Harrison in his *Wood Warblers' World.* The latter family is one to which our tiny gnatcatchers belong, and most are much less brilliantly colored. Later, it became clear that the exclusively New World "warblers" were taxonomically quite different, but the name was by that time firmly established. Thus, the name "wood warbler" was coined, says Harrison, because most are woodland residents.

While quibbling over the finer points of avian nomenclature, it might also be appropriate to note that very few of these birds actually warble. Many are less-than-gifted musicians, and their repertoire consists mainly of an assortment of buzzes, chips, whistles, and trills ranging up and down the scale. They are persistent and cheerful singers, and their concerts always prove welcome on warm spring days, but they cannot compete with such accomplished vocalists as the thrushes, orioles, grosbeaks, and buntings.

Canada warbler

The wood warblers are, however, widespread and dazzlingly beautiful. Their diverse color patterns glitter like Christmas ornaments atop the trees in the midst of migration fallouts along the Texas coast. Flying in loose flocks across the Gulf of Mexico, the birds may reach our shores exhausted, especially if bucking strong headwinds or bone-chilling rains. Then they drop from the sky by the hundreds, filling woodlands and urban backyards with the entire spectrum of colorful hues. Such occasions provide the highlights of any birder's year. It is not unusual to encounter 25 species of warblers in one day; we have seen a dozen in a single tree, each arrayed in flamboyant finery.

There are about 110 species of warblers (birders quickly drop the "wood" as a matter of both provincialism and convenience). Exclusively residents of the New World, as we have noted, they occur throughout North, Central, and South America and the West Indies.

Some, like the yellow warbler, in all its various color forms and subspecies, has a very large range through temperate zones to the tropics. Others are extremely local. The little black-and-white elfin-woods warbler, for example, inhabits only the high mountain forests of Puerto Rico and was not discovered until 1971.

The rare Kirtland's warbler, a severely endangered species, nests only among young jack-pine thickets in north-central Michigan and winters in the Bahamas. Bachman's warbler, our rarest, is seen only occasionally in remote swamplands of the Southeast. *(The latter species may now be extinct.)*

Texas, too, has its warbler specialties. The Colima warbler, a Mexican species, nests in the United States only in the Chisos Mountains of Big Bend National Park, and the entire world's population of the lovely golden-cheeked warbler breeds on the Edwards Plateau in the central portion of the state.

About 55 warbler species occur in the United States, many passing through the southern states to nest far north in Canada. Others remain in the thickets and forests of the Deep South. A few range coast to coast, but most warblers fall into groups of almost exclusively eastern or western species.

Texas, with its size and habitat diversity, attracts most of the North American warblers, some 50 species. Those of the Houston area and the coastal plain are typically ones that funnel through the eastern states; those of the Hill Country and Trans-Pecos are more likely to be western ones.

Some do not have the word *warbler* in their official names. The ovenbird, Louisiana and northern waterthrushes, yellow-breasted chat, and common yellowthroat are all considered members of the family. Peterson has called them "aberrant species," for they are nonconformists in many of their habits and physical attributes.

Although we have extolled the beauty of the group, there are, in fact, a few who wear only somber shades of brown or gray year-round, and in autumn, when they stream back through Texas to seek the insect riches of more tropical lands, most will be in even duller fall plumage. Their ranks are then swelled, too, by nondescript immature birds hatched that year.

In spring, however, our wood warblers are at their best, and we can only echo Maynard's words in profound appreciation: "Throughout the world we find no finer group of birds."

Living on the Edge: 1991

Hummingbirds delight everyone with their bright, iridescent plumage and constantly whirring wings. These tiny gems, however, live on the edge, constantly searching for food to fuel their incredibly high metabolisms. They perch frequently to rest and preen, but soon zoom off again, visiting flower after flower to sip at nectar reservoirs.

According to Dr. Peter Scott of Arizona State University *(now at Indiana State University)*, the amount of nectar obtained from a single flower is surprisingly small. It is barely enough to be profitable. In return, the hummingbirds carry pollen from one flower to another. But, said Scott in a recent talk on "The Interaction of Hummingbirds and Plants" at the Rockport-Fulton Hummer/Bird Celebration, they are relatively inefficient from the plant's point of view. Hummingbirds provide only a "half-decent pollination service." These two factors shape the behavior and natural selection of both parties. Most interactions are mutually beneficial.

Flower nectar consists primarily of a solution of sugar in water. There may also be trace minerals and amino acids, but these are usually scarce in typical hummingbird plants. Most of the birds' energy comes from this nectar.

In his research on Lucifer hummingbirds in Texas' Big Bend, Scott found that they devoted 90 percent of their feeding time to obtaining nectar. The remaining 10 percent was spent hawking insects and spiders, which supply necessary protein. In laboratory experiments with caged birds, Scott also discovered they burned about eight kilocalories of energy each day. Because one gram of sugar provides four kilocalories, a hummingbird requires two grams of sugar a day.

Scott next used micropipettes to extract the minute quantities of nectar produced by various desert flowers and found that nectar averaged about 30 percent sugar by weight. Each flower provided slightly more than a milligram, barely enough to fuel the continuing search

Lucifer hummingbird

for sustenance. From these figures, Scott then calculated that a hummingbird needs nectar from about two thousand flowers a day to balance its energy budget, and that is optimistic, because many plants are visited by other hungry diners first. A more realistic total is probably five thousand flower visits each and every day.

Why don't plants increase their nectar production to encourage more hummingbird visits? Nectar is costly to produce, and the available sugar must also go to other purposes, including growth and seed production. The plant must balance its reward of nectar with its other needs. The hummingbird, in turn, must forage as efficiently as possible. It would stay with a plant that produced more nectar, but that would not help the plant in its quest for pollination. "There is a basic conflict of interest," Scott points out.

The common and widespread trumpet-creeper does produce ten times as much nectar as most other hummingbird plants, yet it makes demands in return for the abundant reward. The feeding bird must literally dive headlong into the large, tubular flowers, where pollen is efficiently pressed onto its crown.

Hummingbirds in the Rocky Mountains employ various feeding strategies, depending on their physical abilities. The feisty rufous hummingbird stakes out a territory and defends patches of its favorite blooms, expending less energy in its search for food. The smaller, less aggressive calliope hummingbird roams over a larger area, feeding at widely scattered plants. The calliope makes its liv-

Our Life with Birds

ing on the run, from plants not worth defending. Because of these wide-ranging tactics, it serves as a better pollinator.

"The sugar reward is barely profitable for hummingbirds," says Scott. "It's in the plants' best interests to keep hummingbirds lean and hungry and moving around." It is a delicate balance that has evolved for the benefit of both.

Naturalist John Muir said it best: "When one tugs at a single thing in nature, he finds it attached to the rest of the world."

The lives of our myriad plants and animals are linked and intertwined in an enormously complex web of life. Some of the links are immediately obvious, but many are far more subtle. Changing one component of an ecosystem will eventually affect all the rest.

In his hummingbird research, for example, Dr. Peter Scott noted that nectar is a reward plants offer in return for pollination; they provide no more than necessary to attract a pollinator. There is always a basic conflict of interest between plant and hummingbird, yet their fates are intricately linked. This relationship is further complicated by other actors in the ongoing drama. Each partner has competitors for its services; there are many nectar sources and many potential pollinators.

Lucifer hummingbirds arrive in Texas' Big Bend in the spring and breed in the arroyos and rocky canyon mouths around the Chisos Mountains. One of the most abundant plants of that environment is the spiny ocotillo, yet Scott seldom saw hummingbirds visiting the flowers of that plant. Why, he wondered, should that be the case? The bright red orange flowers seemed a perfect nectar source, and his measurements showed them to produce normal quantities of sugar. Moreover, the tubular flower shape is usually favored by hummingbirds, for it excludes bees and other competitors that lack the hummers' long, slender bills and probing tongues.

The culprit, Scott discovered, was a large black carpenter bee. Instead of attempting to crawl into the blooms to feed, the bees pierced the tubes near the base to reach the nectar. When Scott measured the sugar content of the flowers, he found it decreased rapidly with the number of bee slits in the corollas. With no cuts, the flowers contained about two milligrams of sugar; with two cuts, there was little sugar remaining, and the flowers were no longer profitable for the hummingbird. It could not afford to visit them on its never-ending search for food.

This seeming act of nectar piracy does not shortcut the pollination process, for the carpenter bee rubs its abdomen on the anthers projecting above the tube while cutting into it. In fact, Scott found an increase in seed production in flowers with the most bee cuts. Because of this competition, however, there was little reward remaining for the birds. Consequently, Lucifer hummingbirds in Texas' Big Bend seldom visit ocotillo blooms.

In contrast, when Scott investigated similar relationships in the Anza-Borrego Desert of southern California, he found migrating rufous hummingbirds feeding actively at ocotillo blossoms and even defending them against other intruders. In this case, there were no native carpenter bees to pirate away the nectar supply.

Big Bend's bees make their nest burrows by tunneling into the woody flower stalks of the agaves and sotols. There they lay their eggs and provision the nests with a "bee bread" of nectar and pollen to sustain the young. Those agaves and sotols do not occur in the California desert system that includes Anza-Borrego, and thus the carpenter bees are also absent. Without the competition, hummingbirds again find ocotillo blossoms to be profitable. It is just one more interesting chapter in the long and tangled story of the birds and the bees.

9

Birds in Peril

Many of our native birds are declining rapidly. Some are included on state and federal lists as threatened or endangered species; others are considered of "special concern" as their numbers dwindle with each passing year. A few, such as the ivory-billed woodpecker, have probably vanished forever, never again to be added to birders' lists, never again to thrill those who walk through the bottomland forests of the southeastern states.

Fortunately, there are success stories, too, and these offer hope in the fight to save our avian heritage. While writing these columns through the years, we have witnessed the return of the brown pelican to the Texas coast and have followed increasing populations of bald eagles and whooping cranes.

We can still thrill to the colorful plumage and wheezy song of the golden-cheeked warbler, but the courtship dance of Attwater's prairie-chicken has been stilled in all but a tiny remnant of its former range. The key, of course, is habitat conservation, whether for our resident birds or for the Neotropical migrants that brave phenomenal journeys twice a year. All warrant our concern; all offer a great deal of enjoyment as we encounter them along our nature trails.

The Native Texan—Golden-cheeked Warbler: 1984/1990

Among the hundreds of bird species that range across the state, only one is uniquely Texan. The little golden-cheeked warbler is the only bird that nests exclusively in Texas and nowhere else, migrating southward to spend the winter in Central America. Unfortunately, this little gem, attired in golden yellow, black, and white, has also earned a place of dubious distinction on the endangered species list and is in great peril in the only nesting range it knows.

The golden-cheek was first listed on an emergency basis on May 4, 1990, because of severe threats to its environment. Under the emergency rule, it was given complete protection of the Endangered Species Act for a period of 240 days. At the same time, the process was begun to list the species under normal procedures. *(That listing was subsequently completed and remains in force today.)*

Golden-cheeked warblers inhabit mature juniper-oak woodlands that cover the rugged slopes and canyons of the Edwards Plateau in Central Texas, an area that encompasses some of Texas' most scenic state parks, including Pedernales Falls, Guadalupe River, Lost Maples, and Meridian. This nesting range is one of the most restricted of any North American bird.

The tiny warblers begin arriving on these breeding grounds in

Golden-cheeked warbler

Our Life with Birds

early March from their winter homes in Guatemala, Honduras, and Nicaragua, flying across the mountains of the Sierra Madre Oriental in Mexico. Males arrive first, to be followed in a few days by the females. Here they rear their single brood and depart again by July or early August.

Somewhere along their evolutionary pathway, golden-cheeks acquired the compulsive need to construct their nests of strips of bark from mature Ashe juniper trees. Neither bark from young trees nor that from any other species of juniper seems to be acceptable, and thus the birds are confined to habitats in which Ashe juniper predominates. It is an amazing dependence on a single environmental niche.

Like many other juniper species across the country, Ashe juniper is often called "cedar," although the true cedars are of a different family and are not native to North America. Dense stands of these trees in central Texas are referred to locally as "cedar brakes."

Urban expansion and the clearing of the land threaten a large portion of this habitat. A recent survey reports a loss of from 15 to 45 percent of suitable warbler habitat over a ten-year period (*concluding in 1990*). Satellite imagery also indicates that of approximately fifty-seven thousand acres of suitable habitat remaining, 70 percent is in fragments too small for the birds to use. Hence the emergency edict.

The critical woodlands are found on private, state, and federal lands and are, at least for the time being, secure on the public tracts. However, less than 3 percent of Texas' land is in public hands; thus, conservation depends largely on proper management of private property. With urban sprawl, and as more and more people move into the scenic Texas Hill Country, the most immediate threat to the golden-cheeked warbler stems from commercial and residential development.

Although the warblers require the juniper bark for nesting material, monospecific stands of those trees do not constitute prime golden-cheek habitat. Only mixed woodlands can supply the numerous and varied insects and other invertebrates on which the birds depend for food, both for themselves and for their young. Proper habitat contains a mixed growth of Ashe juniper, several oaks, red-bud, bumelia, Texas ash, escarpment cherry, cedar elm, pecan, Arizona walnut, and other such trees, along with a diversity of grasses, shrubs, vines, and wildflowers. It is to such an environment that the world's population of golden-cheeked warblers comes to perpetuate the species.

Arriving in the spring, males select their territories and announce their claims in song, defending the boundaries against other males. The females, alone, do the work of building nests and incubating the eggs.

The female pulls long strips of bark from mature junipers and weaves the strips into a little cup, frequently using cobwebs to bind them together. The nest is then lined with mammal fur or with feathers. Virtually all of the nests studied have been made in a similar manner, confirming the total dependence on Ashe juniper. The nests, however, are frequently located in oaks or other trees, at an average height of fifteen feet above the ground.

Once the eggs hatch, the male takes an active role in the care and feeding of the young, and his buzzy song, *tweah-tweah-tweesy*, also translated as *bzzzz layzee dayzee*, is heard less frequently. The incubation of the three or four eggs requires twelve days, and the young leave the nest in eight or nine days more, remaining in a family group to be cared for by the parents.

The male golden-cheeked warbler, as his name implies, has a bright yellow cheek strikingly outlined in black, with a prominent black line through the eye. The throat and upperparts are black; the underparts, pure white. Females are olive green with black streaking and lack the black throat. Without careful examination, they might be mistaken for black-throated green warblers of the eastern portion of the state.

The golden-cheek shares portions of its range with the black-capped vireo, another endangered songbird that nests primarily in Texas. Both may be parasitized by the brown-headed cowbird, which lays its eggs in the nests of other birds, but by far the most serious threat lies in loss of critical habitat. Land clearing for agriculture and home building continues to eliminate large tracts of juniper-oak woodland on the Edwards Plateau, much to the detriment of the birds.

Endangered species are indicators of environmental problems. To save the golden-cheeked warbler or the black-capped vireo, we must preserve their unique habitat, and in so doing, we provide a home for countless other animals and plants as well.

Return from the Brink—Brown Pelican: 1997

The welcoming committee is waiting as we approach tiny Sundown Island in Texas' Matagorda Bay on a warm, sunny morning in mid-May. Stately herons and egrets pace the shallows, while hordes of laughing gulls patrol the beach. Large, bulky brown pelicans stand in small groups at the water's edge, launching into ponderous flight as we draw near.

Created from dredge spoil in 1962, the twenty-acre island lies near the intersection of the Matagorda Ship Channel and the Gulf Intracoastal Waterway just east of Port O'Connor. It is leased from the Texas General Land Office and managed by the National Audubon Society's coastal sanctuaries program under the supervision of warden Chester Smith.

Locally called "Bird Island," Sundown is home to eighteen species of colonial waterbirds. As many as twenty-five thousand pairs of gulls, terns, skimmers, herons, spoonbills, ibises, and pelicans nest here each spring and summer, feeding their young on the abundant marine life spawned in the surrounding wetlands.

Brown pelican

All are important to this coastal ecosystem; all are fascinating to see. However, the brown pelicans provide the focal point of our trip, for we have never before encountered these great birds on their nesting grounds in Texas.

The endangered brown pelican all but disappeared from the Texas and Louisiana coasts during the 1950s and 1960s, the victim of DDT and other pesticides. It shared the fate of the bald eagle, osprey, and peregrine falcon, other bird species at the top of their food chains. Incorporating the persistent chemicals into their body tissues, they were unable to lay viable eggs.

Over the last few years, brown pelicans have staged a remarkable comeback, once again nesting on islands in the bays and patrolling the shoreline on broad, seven-foot wings. From a small colony of sixty pairs in 1989, the population on Sundown Island has increased steadily through the decade. A meticulous census in 1996 counted 1,132 pelican nests and, although this year's (1997) official count has not yet been taken, Smith estimates there will be as many as two thousand pairs of the giant birds. It is a spectacle beyond belief.

From the boat, we see pelicans perched atop the low shrubbery that dots the island. Others are hidden away in the waist-high grasses and amid dense stands of silverleaf sunflowers that cover this portion of the sandy refuge. Large signs ringing the island proclaim its status as an Audubon sanctuary and prohibit landing during the nesting season. Smith, however, must make his periodic rounds, and we are privileged to join him as he wades ashore.

Laughing gulls swirl around us as we walk the beach, their screams proclaiming ownership of tiny patches of sheltered sand along the vegetation line. Handsome in their black-hooded courtship plumage, they are just beginning their nesting cycle.

Farther inland, the pelicans hold sway. Some have built their large nests of dried grasses and plant fibers directly on the ground. Other nests perch atop low baccharis bushes, weighting down the foliage with their considerable bulk. Packed closely together, most now hold downy young.

Even at this tender age, the pale gray chicks are obviously pelicans. Their incongruous bills appear much too large for their slender necks, and occasionally the top-heavy birds fall abruptly on their faces as they attempt to sit upright in the nest. They would win no adolescent beauty pageants, but they will rapidly outgrow this awkward age.

The adults are elegantly dressed in full breeding plumage, their gleaming white heads lightly tinged with yellow, the backs of their necks a rich chestnut brown. Brownish gray wings gleam silvery in the bright sunlight, and ivory yellow patches ornament the birds' enormous beaks. Even the facial skin glows with hormonal color at this season of the year.

From close range we watch the pelicans as they brood their new hatchlings to shield them from the penetrating sun. When any seem nervous or poised for flight, we back quickly away so they are not distracted from their parental duties. Careless intruders can cause irreparable harm in a nesting colony by keeping the birds from their nests as eggs and babies perish in the sun or fall prey to gulls and other predators.

Enthralled, we watch as the parents feed their young. Stubby, featherless little wings flailing wildly, straining to stand upright on still-shaky legs, the babies stretch to reach far into the adult's pouch. Some seem almost to dive headlong into the gaping gullet. Ornithologist Terence Shortt vividly described such a scene as "like a wrestling match, and the writhing and contorting are both alarming and revolting." The half-digested fishy soup that the parents regurgitate and drip into the probing beaks does not look appetizing by human standards, but the two or three young vie vigorously for extra portions.

All too soon, it is time to leave, and as we walk slowly down the beach, we stop often to glance back at what is now the largest brown pelican colony on the Texas coast. Clearly, the National Audubon Society and warden Chester Smith have done a remarkable job in maintaining a sanctuary for this majestic endangered species and the others that share its sandy, saline domain.

The sights and sounds of Sundown Island are almost beyond belief. As we walk the beach, accompanying Smith on his regular rounds, hordes of raucous laughing gulls swarm around our heads. A year-round resident, this is the only gull that remains on the Texas coast to breed when others move northward with the spring. Now, in mid-May, they are just beginning to stake their claims to spots along the vegetation line. Some have built crude nests of weed stems and debris; others will lay their three spotted, olive eggs directly on the ground. In 1996, these handsome, black-hooded gulls numbered an astonishing ten thousand pairs, the most numerous of all the Sundown birds.

On down the shore, Smith points out a closely packed group of black skimmers on an open, barren patch of sand. These, too, are just settling down to nest, although a few of the birds sit tightly as if already incubating their three to five spotted eggs. Not wanting to disturb the colony, we watch for a time through binoculars and then return to our anchored boat.

Wading ashore on the opposite end of the island, we find an assortment of other birds. Great blue herons perch atop the vegetation, haughtily standing their ground at our approach. Others flap slowly and sedately past on enormous wings.

Smaller tricolored and little blue herons dot the low, windswept salt-cedar *(more properly known as tamarisk)*, baccharis, and spiny hackberry trees like Christmas ornaments, while great egrets and snowy egrets parade through the dense stands of silverleaf sunflower, the latter flashing their distinctive "golden slippers." All participate in the guttural chorus of grunts and groans that passes for heron conversation.

With a loud squawk, a black-crowned night-heron leaps into flight from a hackberry close beside us. Its long, slender white plumes trail back from the dark crown in an elegant display.

Other night-herons perch nearby, and we also pick out occasional white-faced and white ibises with their strange, down-curved bills. The white-faced ibis is dark chestnut brown glossed with iridescent green and purple, a thin white line bordering the bare facial skin. Immaculately white with black wing tips, the white ibis has a pink face and beak that flushes with red hormonal color in the heat of springtime passion.

All are occupied with courtship or nesting, but none more intently than a group of reddish egrets. One by one, these handsome, long-legged birds rustle their wings and erect the plumes on their heads and necks, twisting and turning in the afternoon sun. Others answer in kind, a mutual display that needs no translation. To the pageant winners go mates and nesting territories; nothing else matters at this time of year.

A seriously threatened species, the reddish egret occurs in North America primarily in southern Florida and along the Texas coast. It, like the brown pelican, requires isolated island rookeries if it is to continue to survive, for it seldom wanders inland from the shore.

Many of these herons and their relatives already have crude nests cradled among the branches of the low trees, some almost touching adjacent nests. There is no discrimination in this avian tenement; the birds mix freely with other species. Most lay unmarked light bluish green eggs distinguishable only by their size.

Some eggs, however, stand out from all the rest. Laid in crude stick nests lined with dead leaves, their dirty white shells are heavily splotched with brown. These are the eggs of the roseate spoonbills, which stand calmly watching as we slowly make our rounds. What these birds lack in facial beauty with their naked heads and bizarre,

Black-crowned night-heron

spatulate beaks, they more than make up for in elegant pink plumage. Now they also wear brilliant crimson epaulettes and flash bright orange tails as they posture before their mates. Only the most phlegmatic observer could fail to be impressed.

Farther on down the island, we see another bare patch of sand, and here we find a very different kind of nesting colony. Large, orange-billed royal terns and smaller, black-billed Sandwich terns crowd in shoulder to shoulder, their tiny territories just out of pecking range of the nearest neighbors. There are thousands of these graceful, streamlined birds just settling down to their seasonal chores, and we approach no closer for fear of disturbing them. Peering cautiously over a slight rise, we admire them from afar and then slowly back away.

In caring for his twenty-five thousand pairs of feathered tenants, Smith faces many challenges and threats to their well-being. Hurricane winds and tidal surges wipe out low-lying nests, and constant wave action slowly erodes the sandy beaches. In 1994, forty nests of the threatened reddish egret were lost to an infestation of imported fire ants. Now Smith laboriously barges a tractor to the island in early spring and again in fall, broadcasting granules of fire-ant bait to save his birds.

Careless humans, too, occasionally land in spite of large signs that expressly forbid trespass during the nesting season, thereby wreaking havoc on delicate eggs and young.

Suitable habitat for our beautiful and varied coastal birds is in increasingly short supply, and Sundown Island remains an invaluable gem astride the busy waterways of Matagorda Bay.

When the authors first began birding in 1962, brown pelicans were virtually gone from the Texas coast. Only through legislation banning the persistent pesticides that interfered with the reproductive process were they brought back to an ecosystem they once populated in huge numbers. Their fate is by no means secure, however, and their continued success depends on the preservation of such vital habitats as Sundown Island. At the same time, those habitats serve countless other avian species, many of which are also declining in the face of human intrusion.

Our National Bird—Bald Eagle: 1997

The huge nest of sticks fills the top of a tall, slender pine, its massive shape cradled by the upper tier of branches that fan out above to provide a canopy of dappled shade. Two large, dark birds perch on the rim of the nest, occasionally flapping their wings rhythmically, sometimes even lifting a few inches into the air before settling down again to rest. Relaxing, they carefully rearrange and preen feathers ruffled by this vigorous morning exercise.

At first glance, one might assume the birds to be hawks, but they are much too large. Their wings seem extraordinarily wide when spread and span more than seven feet; their enormous beaks are sharply hooked. These spectacular birds are young bald eagles. In a few more days they will leave their aerie to fly free above the surrounding river-bottom woodlands and fish in the adjacent lakes.

It is a scene one might expect in the far-flung forests of Alaska or northern Minnesota, but such is not the case. This nest adorns the top of a loblolly pine in Chambers County north of Galveston Bay. The eagles are native-born Texans, members of a nonmigratory population that will remain in our state throughout the year.

We have not ventured far into the wilderness to achieve our vantage point. We watch from a friend's backyard as these eaglets pose unconcerned. Hidden from a nearby road by a narrow screen of trees, the adult pair has nested within view of human habitation for four or five years.

Bald eagles return to the same site year after year, adding new material to the stick nest until it reaches incredible proportions. One such nest proved to be nearly ten feet across and twenty feet deep; another weighed more than two tons and contained branches six feet long and several inches in diameter. Perched high in the tops of trees, these enormous structures sometimes plummet to earth as the trees snap under the accumulated weight.

The nest we watch is relatively new and has not yet reached such epic size. It is huge, nonetheless, and the eagles appear deceptively small as they clamber about on the wide rim.

The female bald eagle lays from one to three large bluish white eggs each season. The normal clutch is two, but because the chicks hatch at different times, the firstborn has a distinct advantage, and the second sometimes dies. Incubation requires from thirty-four to thirty-six days, with both parents taking their turns, and the young are about three months old before they leave the security of the nest.

The white head and tail of the adult bald eagle make it immediately recognizable. Immatures, however, are mostly dark, with irregular white patches in the wings and at the base of the tail. They do not attain adult plumage until their fourth year and can easily be confused with the golden eagle of the western states or with large, dark hawks.

Texas' small resident population of bald eagles nests along the coastal plain between Corpus Christi and the Houston-Galveston area and on some of the larger wooded lakes and reservoirs in the eastern portion of the state. Because our national bird is still listed as a threatened species, all of the nesting pairs are kept under close observation by state and federal biologists.

Bald eagle

Winter brings down a larger number of eagles from the North to supplement the local population. Some move onto the lakes in eastern and central Texas, where they feed primarily on fish. Others hunt on the coastal prairies, surviving on wounded ducks and geese left by their human counterparts. A winter census earlier this year (1997) counted 305 bald eagles on twenty-two Texas lakes, but most returned northward with the spring. Only a few remained in our state to nest and rear their young.

It is a warm, clear March morning as we watch the nest in Chambers County. An hour passes with little activity, and then we hear a shrill, distant cry. Both young eaglets are instantly alert, and we turn to see an adult eagle flying toward us with a fish clutched securely in its talons. Again it screams, an absurdly high-pitched call for so large a predator. It sweeps past us quickly and swoops up to drop its catch into the nest, alighting on the rim as its young immediately attack the fish.

The brief meal over, both parent and young settle down again to bask in the sun. Then, to our surprise, another white head rises above the bowl of sticks. The second adult has been hidden from view the entire time, apparently resting deep inside the nest. It, too, joins the others perched around the rim.

It is the first time we have ever watched an entire eagle family, and we thrill to the spectacle. The young continue their periodic exercise, while their parents stand quietly, occasionally preening or stretching their wings. Hours pass with little activity.

Finally, one of the adults drops suddenly from the nest and sails away toward a nearby lake. A few minutes later, the other leaves in similar fashion, and the eaglets are left alone and unattended.

We continue our vigil, but the adults do not return. The sun drops slowly behind the pines, and we finally prepare to leave. Looking back one more time, we see the two young bald eagles perched high on their aerie. It has been an exciting day with one of the rarest and most magnificent of Texas' avian residents.

Texas' bald eagles continue to prosper. According to a note by Brent Ortego and Chris Gregory of the Texas Parks and Wildlife Department in a 2003 Bulletin of the Texas Ornithological Society, *there were 54 active eagle nests within the state in 1997. By 2002, that number had increased to 110. A total of 153 young eagles fledged from 93 of those occupied nests.*

Birders place a high priority on finding species they have never seen before. Adding new birds to the list is part of the game, and such lifers engender great excitement for experienced birders and novices alike. Certainly, it is thrilling to see something new, but even the more common birds provide opportunities for discovery. Each is a creature of enormous complexity; each offers new perspectives on avian life.

In watching the bald eagle family in Chambers County, we marveled again and again at the grandeur of these great birds as both adults and their offspring posed in their treetop nest. It was not the first time we had seen this magnificent species, yet that day with the eagles will long remain in our minds. It is one more vivid vignette of a beautiful and fascinating bird.

Another such magical moment occurred two years ago and fifteen hundred miles away. Paddling slowly down a Minnesota river in a canoe, we listened to American bitterns calling from the sedges along the bank and veeries singing vespers from the nearby forest. A beaver swam past, towing an aspen branch to its lodge. Hundreds of shimmering dragonflies basked in the last rays of the setting sun.

Then, two large birds sailed toward us on broad, flat wings. The golden light gleamed on the snow white heads and tails, marking them as adult bald eagles. Another adult joined them, and the trio swooped low over the water in search of fish, passing no more than thirty feet above us as we rested on our paddles and stared in awe.

The eagle pair settled together into the top of a towering pine across the marsh, while the other chose a leaning birch on the opposite bank. There they remained, majestic and serene, as we finally turned in the twilight and reluctantly paddled out of sight.

Yet another encounter proved to be one of the highlights on a trip to Washington's Olympic Peninsula. Standing on the sheer cliffs of Cape Flattery, we faced the Strait of Juan de Fuca to the north and the blue Pacific to the west. The view alone was worth the trip.

Our Life with Birds

Flocks of sooty shearwaters flew just above the waves, while common murres and black guillemots paddled about in the onshore waters. On the rocks below, black oystercatchers and surfbirds scurried back and forth amid orange and purple starfish and green sea anemones.

Looking across a narrow cove to another precipice, we spotted a tufted puffin standing on a moss-covered ledge. The chunky, charcoal gray bird had curling yellow plumes framing its white face, and its absurdly heavy, triangular orange bill gave it a strangely comical expression. It was a bird we had long wanted to find, one we had never seen before.

In the midst of all these uniquely western birds, all eyes suddenly turned upward as an adult bald eagle flew low above the trees. Another joined it in a swirling aerial display, and together they glided past us, braking sharply and sweeping up to settle into the upper branches of a towering cliffside Douglas-fir. There they perched in profile, face-to-face, the two birds filling the field of our binoculars, providing the ultimate view of our national bird.

Not all our memories of eagles are quite so regal. Exploring Florida's Everglades several years ago, we chanced upon a young bald eagle eating a fish on the lawn of a fishing camp. A light rain was slanting down on a stiff breeze off the bay, and the bird's dark plumage was ruffled and dripping.

Lured by the eagle's catch, two fish crows cautiously approached and attempted to steal a bite. At each sortie, however, the much larger eagle turned to face the thieves, flashing its powerful talons and massive, sharply hooked beak.

One of the crows then slipped cautiously up behind the eagle and grasped a tail feather in its beak, giving it a sudden tug. As the eagle whirled on its attacker, the other crow slipped in to steal a bit of fish. It then played the aggressor, while its partner in crime got a bite to eat. The game went on for several minutes, with the two fish crows alternating in their roles. Finally, they flew off with the remainder of the meal, leaving the bedraggled young eagle standing forlornly in the rain.

While visiting Nebraska's Platte River early last spring to see the migration of the sandhill cranes, we spotted three large birds sitting together in a bare cottonwood tree beside the river. We quickly set up a spotting scope and discovered them to be bald eagles in three very different plumages.

One bird was a handsome adult, with white head and tail and gleaming yellow bill and feet. Another was an immature eagle in dark blackish brown plumage, its chest flecked sparingly with white. The remaining bird had white spreading diffusely through the tail, and its head was mostly white. A wide, dark line running through the eye, however, gave it a strangely ospreylike appearance. This was a three-year-old eagle just approaching adulthood. In another year it would gain its characteristic white head and tail.

All three birds were visible together in the scope, giving us an incomparable look at the progression of plumages. This, too, provided an indelible vignette in our overall experience with bald eagles that ranges from Texas to Minnesota and from Washington to Florida. We never tire of seeing new aspects of each bird's habits and personality. This is one of the real thrills of birding, especially when that subject is one that is slowly recovering from its status as a severely endangered species.

Love Affair with a Great White Bird—Whooping Crane:
1980/1990

The tall, stately birds stride across the coastal marsh, stopping occasionally to pluck a tasty morsel from the shallow water. The two adults are plumaged in immaculate white, their elongated tertial feathers forming the "bustle" that gives cranes their distinctive shape. Their slightly smaller youngster is still washed and mottled with rusty brown.

One of the parents catches a blue crab and drops it up on the muddy bank, where the juvenile grabs it and wolfs it down. They wander a little farther and then launch themselves into the air. Wings spanning seven feet beat ponderously, revealing for the first time the black wing tips that are hidden except in flight. Long necks are outstretched in typical crane fashion; legs trail far out behind. Across the marsh comes the trumpeting call, *ker-loo ker-lee-loo,* an echo from the Pleistocene, resonating within the five-foot windpipes of these tallest of all North American birds.

The recovery of the whooping crane is one of the brightest success stories in North American conservation. The plight of this species has been followed around the world, and the effort to save it has been called "a love affair of two nations with a great white bird."

At one time, the whooper ranged across the continent. Widespread, but probably never abundant, the species gave way to the advancing human settlers of the land. Many birds were shot for food or trophies; others vanished as their marshlands were drained and cleared. When President Franklin D. Roosevelt signed an executive order creating the new federal Aransas Migratory Waterfowl Refuge on December 31, 1937, only two small flocks of whooping cranes remained. One flock migrated south from Canada to winter at Aransas. The other remained year-round in Louisiana.

The latter flock, containing a dozen cranes, was decimated by a tropical storm in 1940, and the few remaining birds disappeared one by one within the next few years. The new Texas refuge, now known as the Aransas National Wildlife Refuge, provided a haven for all that were left. The fate of the whooping crane rested on a tiny remnant of fifteen birds.

The nesting ground of these migratory cranes was not known until 1954. After several searches had failed, a forester and helicopter pilot flying to a wildfire spotted adults with young along the Sass River in Wood Buffalo National Park in the Northwest Territories. Since then, Canadian and U.S.

Whooping crane

biologists have been able to study the whooping cranes on their breeding grounds and to follow them on their annual migration of some twenty-four hundred miles between northern Canada and the Texas coast.

Whooping cranes lay two eggs, but only one chick normally survives. Thus, at little risk to the wild population, the biologists began in 1967 to remove one egg from some of the nests in order to raise a captive flock at the Patuxent Research Center of the U.S. Fish and Wildlife Service in Laurel, Maryland.

In 1975, another experiment began in which whooping crane eggs were placed in the nests of sandhill cranes at Idaho's Grays Lake Refuge. This practice continued for several years and seemed at first to have great potential. The fledgling whoopers migrated with their foster-parent sandhill cranes from Idaho to refuges in New Mexico; however, they showed no interest in mating with others of their kind as they reached adulthood, and they gradually succumbed to accidents and predators. The experiment was finally terminated, and captive flocks are now being maintained at Patuxent and at the International Crane Foundation in Baraboo, Wisconsin.

The migratory flock wintering in Texas, meanwhile, began to increase slowly but steadily with added protection and concern. From a low of 15 in 1941, the population passed 100 in 1986. In the fall of 1990, a record 146 whooping cranes arrived on the Texas coast from Canada, but only 134 survived to make the return journey. At least one was shot; others apparently died of natural causes or were killed by predators.

The future is much brighter than it was a half century ago, but the fate of the whooping crane is by no means assured. "It is reassuring to look at what has happened over the past few years," said Brent Giezentanner, manager of the Aransas Refuge, in a 1990 interview with the *New York Times*, "but people should not be too reassured because the whoopers are fifteen minutes from catastrophe every day they spend down here." Loss of habitat to coastal erosion, dredging, poisonous contaminants in the soil and water, and possible oil or chemical spills in the Intracoastal Canal that cleaves the refuge all threaten the flock.

On a recent trip from Rockport, Texas, aboard Captain Ted Appell's boat, *The Skimmer*, to see the cranes, we also passed several chemical barges traversing the feeding grounds of the endangered birds. One tug was pushing two barges loaded with two million gallons of flammable, toxic benzene. About three thousand barges a year pass through this busy waterway, and all pass within sight of the cranes. "The question is not whether a barge collision is going to occur, but when," says Giezentanner.

The cranes begin arriving at Aransas Refuge in late October and remain into April. Migrating as family groups, they set up territories of nearly a square mile in the coastal marsh and stalk through the shallows to feed on blue crabs, clams, and occasional small fish. Acorns, berries, roots, and grains supplement the varied diet. The long-legged cranes roost standing in shallow water, where it is more difficult for predators to approach.

Cranes can sometimes be seen from the observation tower at Aransas, and a number of boats docked in the Rockport-Fulton area offer crane-watching trips. The boats guarantee seeing a number of cranes, and close-up views are frequent. Few experiences in Texas birding equal a personal encounter with the majestic whooping cranes, and few who see them fail to fall in love with these great white birds.

Conservation efforts continue for the whooping cranes, and the population continues to build slowly. During the winter of 1999–2000, a record 188 birds visited Aransas, but by the spring of 2002, that number had declined again to 174. The high mortality apparently correlated with the scarcity of blue crabs on the Texas coast. This, in turn, resulted from the severe summer drought of 2000 and the lack of freshwater inflows essential to the productivity of marine species in the bays and estuaries. Numbers will obviously fluctuate from year to year, hopefully with an overall upward trend.

As this population increases, however, habitat must be found for the new families of cranes. Some have now moved off the refuge to seek their own territories for feeding and roosting. Smaller parcels of land are being purchased and added to Aransas Refuge, and private landowners must also offer safe harbor for their charges.

In addition, new programs are under way to establish other flocks of whooping cranes. A nonmigratory group introduced gradually in Florida recently succeeded in fledging the first whooping crane hatched in the United States in decades, and another migratory flock has been created by training young, captive-reared cranes to fly behind an ultralight aircraft between winter habitats in Florida and their summer territory in Wisconsin. Both projects hold great hopes for the dispersal of the whooping cranes across the continent so that the entire population is not subject to a single environmental disaster.

Gone but Not Forgotten—Ivory-billed Woodpecker: 1985

The U.S. Fish and Wildlife Service has recently initiated a status review of the ivory-billed woodpecker to determine whether or not it should be declared officially extinct and removed from the endangered species list. It is the latest of a number of North American wildlife species to reach the brink of extinction because of human activities.

Declared endangered on the first such list issued by the Service in 1967, this largest of our woodpeckers has been reported periodically across the Southeast. However, these reports have never been verified and must be regarded, at least in part, as cases of mistaken identity.

The Department of the Interior review notes, "To the Service's knowledge, there have been no confirmed reports of live ivory-billed woodpeckers since the early 1950's." The Audubon Society *Master Guide to Birding* states, "Recent reports of sightings in the United States have not been substantiated, and the species must be presumed to be extinct on our continent."

A second subspecies, the Cuban ivory-billed woodpecker, may also be extinct and is considered under the current review. The Cuban subspecies historically ranged across most of the island and was nesting through the 1950s in the pine forests of the eastern mountains. Efforts to find it in recent years have proved unsuccessful.

The enormous ivory-bill averages about twenty inches in length, with a wing span of nearly three feet. It is shiny black with white stripes down the neck from cheek to back. Large white areas on the upper surface of the wings are seen as a white triangular patch across the bird's back, clearly visible when it perches on a tree trunk. In flight, the patches show as broad borders on the rear edges of the wings. The bird's name derives from its large bill of a distinctly pale ivory color. Both sexes sport a flaring crest—the male's, bright red; the female's, black. The call is a nasal *kent,* quite different from that of other woodpeckers and sounding much like that of an oversized nuthatch.

This extremely rare, and now possibly nonexistent, bird is frequently confused with the relatively common pileated woodpecker. The latter ranges across much of forested North America, from northwestern Canada to Nova Scotia and south to central California, eastern Texas, the Gulf States, and Florida. It is frequently seen in the Houston area, even in wooded urban parks and suburban backyards.

Although smaller than the ivory-bill, the pileated still looms large by woodpecker standards. Averaging seventeen to nineteen inches in length, with a thirty-inch wingspan, it is a formidable, crow-sized bird.

The pileated woodpecker lacks the broad white border at the rear of the wing and, at most, displays smaller white areas at the base of the primaries. Thus, it appears largely black when perched, with only white stripes across the cheeks and down the sides of the neck. In flight, it displays white wing linings beneath, whereas the ivory-bill has white on both the linings and the trailing wing edges. Both sexes of the common pileated woodpecker exhibit red crests. The bill is dark but may shine in the sunlight to appear much lighter to the casual observer.

It is primarily the confusion between the two species that leaves the status of the ivory-bill still in question. Most reports come from novices unaware of the identification problems and of the improbability of finding a surviving ivory-billed woodpecker in any but the most remote timbered habitats.

Ivory-billed woodpecker

We frequently receive calls about purported ivory-bill sightings, and frankly, we are less than enthusiastic about trying to confirm them. We are resigned to the fact that we will almost certainly never see this most magnificent of woodpeckers. On the other hand, we have acquaintances who feel strongly that they have either seen or heard one or more of the rare birds. Most of these reports are carefully guarded on the assumption that the birds are better protected if no one learns of their continued presence. Certainly, an accessible ivory-bill would be plagued by well-intentioned birders seeking to add it to their lists.

Historically, the ivory-billed woodpecker ranged from Illinois to North Carolina and southward into Texas and Florida. Although it was occasionally seen in pine forests bordering the cypress swamps of Florida, it was primarily a bird of the river bottoms and swamps, inhabiting virgin forests of sweet gum, oak, ash, and hackberry.

Our Life with Birds

Apparently never really plentiful, it was hunted by Native Americans who prized the great white bills. According to eighteenth-century naturalist Mark Catesby, "The bills of these birds are much valued by the Canada Indians, who make coronets of 'em for their princes and great warriors, by fixing them round a wreath, with their points outward. The Northern Indians having none of these birds in their cold country, purchase them of the Southern People at the price of two, and sometimes three buck-skins a bill."

White settlers continued the hunt for the spectacular ivory beaks, and early collectors of museum specimens also contributed to a steady population decline. It was ultimately a loss of suitable habitat, however, that spelled doom for the giant woodpeckers.

Unlike other species with more diverse feeding habits, the over-specialized ivory-bill was dependent, at least during the breeding season, on the larvae of large wood-boring beetles. Such larvae are found primarily in mature, recently dead trees or in those damaged by storm or fire.

To ensure the presence of enough mature trees in the proper stage of decay to attract beetles, large tracts of timber were required. Thus, lumbering in the South spelled the end for the species, for the young trees that replaced the virgin forests contained little food for the voracious ivory-bills.

According to Harry Oberholser's encyclopedic work *The Bird Life of Texas,* the first mention of the ivory-billed woodpecker in our state was by John James Audubon. In 1837, he noted that these birds were "abundant" in what is now Harris and Fort Bend Counties. However, even as they were discovered, they were apparently declining rapidly.

By 1918, virtually all of the lowland hardwood forests throughout the South had been logged. There were a few sightings of ivory-bills east of the Trinity River in the 1930s, and ornithologists Arthur Allen and James Tanner described a nesting colony in the wild Singer Tract of northern Louisiana during that same decade. In 1963, a diligent search of the Singer Tract found no sign of the woodpeckers.

The 1960s brought a revival of Texas ivory-bill reports and rumors. Oberholser speculated that "perhaps a few birds had wandered in from Louisiana to take advantage of freshly drowned timber back of newly constructed dams."

Veteran birder Whitney Eastman reported seeing two pairs and a lone female between the Trinity and Neches Rivers in 1960 and 1961, and additional sightings were made in the same area in 1963. In 1966, John Dennis, an authority on woodpeckers, and Houstonian Armand Yramategui reported an ivory-bill near Evadale in the Neches River bottomlands. Countless other birders and naturalists swarmed across the Big Thicket in hopes of seeing the rare bird. Many carried large camera lenses and broadcast taped ivory-bill calls recorded on the Singer Tract three decades earlier.

After years of ornithological furor, there was still no unquestionable evidence of the ivory-billed woodpecker's continued existence. No new photos or sound recordings were obtained. Some searchers reported an abnormally plumaged pileated woodpecker whose additional white feathers made it appear more like its rare relative. The controversy raged on.

"By the early 1970's," Oberholser noted, "Yramategui had been murdered by robbers in Houston and even the indefatigable Dennis *(now also dead)* was discouraged. The search, for the most part, shifted elsewhere. An Ivorybill feather was found in Florida in 1969, but how old was the feather? In South Carolina in 1970, an Ivorybill—or another tape recorder?—answered a taped call, but the bird was not seen. In Louisiana in 1971, two photographs—perhaps of a stuffed bird?—were made by a mysterious photographer in an undisclosed part of the state."

The ivory-billed woodpecker may still exist somewhere in a remote bottomland forest in East Texas or elsewhere across the southeastern states. But if it does, its future is far from secure, and we do not expect to see one during our remaining years of birding.

As recently as April 1999, a seemingly credible sighting of an ivory-billed woodpecker was made in the Pearl River Wildlife Management Area near Slidell, Louisiana, by David Kulivan, a graduate student at Louisiana State University. A subsequent intensive search by a team of ornithologists and experienced birders, however, failed to come up with additional evidence. Likewise, recent observations of the Cuban ivory-bill are lacking, and there is no irrefutable evidence at this time that the species still exists. Certainly, others will continue the search, and there will undoubtedly be more reports of this largest of our woodpeckers. Most, at least, will be the result of wishful thinking.

The Rarest Grouse—Attwater's Prairie-Chicken: 1985/1991/1995/1998

The springtime courtship display of the Attwater's prairie-chicken ranks as one of nature's greatest spectacles. Males patrol their territories in a communal lek, puffing out their orange neck pouches and dancing in competition for the females. Their feet beat the ground so rapidly they are only a blur; the "booming" from the inflated air sacs carries for half a mile in the clear dawn air.

It is a sight we have witnessed many times through the years. We once photographed prairie-chickens from a blind as they danced in the backyard of Mr. and Mrs. J. D. Woodham's Dickinson home in Galveston County and on the concrete runways of nearby Spaceland Airport as small airplanes taxied past. Sometimes the magnificent birds came so close in their wild gyrations that our lenses would no longer focus. Occasionally, they danced on the roof of the blind, and we could only sit and listen.

As novice birders three decades ago, we saw prairie-chickens on Fondren Road in southwest Houston, before roadside fields gave way to unbroken urban sprawl. We encountered them along Highway 146 near Texas City, and there were booming grounds beside Highway 35 south of the little coastal-bend town of Tivoli. At the latter site, we often parked a tour bus on the shoulder of the road and introduced visiting birders to some of Texas' most famous avian citizens. We did not realize at the time how precious those indelible experiences would prove to be. Places that once harbored our favorite flocks are now utterly devoid of the handsome grouse.

Attwater's prairie-chicken is almost gone, the most critically endangered bird in the state. The wild population continues to decline at a perilous rate, and only a captive breeding program offers hope for survival for more than a few years.

Biologists currently regard Attwater's prairie-chicken as a subspecies or race of the greater prairie-chicken, a wide-ranging species found on remnant tallgrass prairies across the Midwest and the Great Plains. The nominate form, too, is now uncommon and local, while another race, the heath hen, vanished from the East Coast in 1932.

Attwater's prairie-chicken was first described by naturalist C. E. Bendire in 1894. At that time, its range extended from Abbeyville, Louisiana, around the coastal bend to at least the Nueces River in southern Texas. An estimated one million birds occupied seven million acres of prairie along the coast. Early accounts tell of flocks that darkened the sky, and the birds were hunted heavily for food and sport until they received protection under modern game laws.

But native tallgrass prairies, this bird's essential habitat, have all but vanished from the coastal plain, giving way to steadily increasing urbanization, ranching, and agriculture. This loss of habitat poses the greatest threat to the remarkable prairie-chicken.

Male Attwater's prairie-chicken displaying

After mating with the amorous males that display in clearings and even in plowed fields, the females steal away to lay their spotted eggs in shallow depressions among the tall, concealing prairie grasses. The clutch varies from seven to as many as seventeen eggs, and reports indicate that the female incubates for twenty-three to twenty-six days. On hatching, the downy, precocial chicks remain with their mother for several weeks, feeding on insects, seeds, berries, and tender leaves.

Prairie-chicken numbers began to drop in the early 1900s as the prairie disappeared and the expanding human population disturbed traditional display and nesting grounds. By 1937, only 8,700 birds were found on forty-five thousand acres.

Attwater's prairie-chicken was officially declared endangered on March 11, 1967, and five years later the eight-thousand-acre Attwater Prairie Chicken National Wildlife Refuge was established near Eagle Lake in Colorado County. At that time, a census found 1,772 birds on the Texas coast. By 1988, that number had dropped to 926; and in 1991, to 480. All that remained were in four major populations in only seven counties.

The question is not "What happened to the prairie-chicken?" noted a status report from the federal refuge. It is "What happened to the prairie?" Only fifteen thousand acres on portions of two refuges were dedicated to the species management—one-fifth of 1 percent of the original seven-million-acre range. Private ranches in Goliad and Refugio Counties provided habitat for 65 percent of the remaining birds, and public education became an essential part of the recovery plan.

On the few remaining prairie tracts, suppression of natural fires ended the succession of native grasses. Trees and brush, once kept under control, crept up from the stream banks. The alien Macartney rose, introduced to Texas from Asia in the 1800s as a windbreak for cattle, also became a serious problem, with the thorny vines covering hundreds of thousands of acres. Not only do the rose thickets encroach on the birds' prairie habitat but they harbor predators such as raccoons and skunks that take a heavy toll of eggs and young.

Introduced fire ants, too, may have contributed to the decline. A serious threat to baby chicks, the voracious ants also displace other insect species that the chicks require as food.

From 1991 through 1993, heavy rainfall during the nesting season resulted in unusually high mortality. The spring of 1994 was relatively dry and offered promise for a successful year, but the wild population had now dropped to 158 individuals in four counties. It plummeted further to only 68 birds in 1995.

Clearly, the only hope of saving the Attwater's prairie-chicken lay in a captive-breeding program that had begun in 1992. Fossil Rim Wildlife Center near Glen Rose was the first facility to successfully propagate prairie-chickens, and Texas A&M University and the Houston Zoo also took up the challenge.

Forty-nine eggs were gathered from nesting areas in Colorado and Galveston Counties in the spring of 1992, and from those eggs, researchers at Fossil Rim produced thirty-five chicks, a nucleus for the breeding program.

Subsequently, the Houston Zoo got two dozen eggs in 1994 from wild flocks near Texas City and in Refugio County. To locate the nests, hens were first captured on the display grounds and fitted with radio transmitters, which then led researchers to the carefully concealed eggs. Like many other species, prairie-chickens often renest if their eggs are destroyed early in the breeding season. It was hoped that the captive flocks could thus be established without unduly affecting the wild population.

Eleven of the first birds in Houston survived to adulthood, and they now form the basis of the zoo's breeding flock. In 1995, one of those females mated with an additional wild-caught adult male and produced eight chicks. Another twelve eggs were obtained from the Refugio County flock and hatched under two brood hens. Two of those chicks were lost, but the Houston Zoo successfully raised eighteen young prairie-chickens, an exceptional success rate.

Chelle Plasse, curator of birds at the Houston Zoo, noted that zoo personnel had first intended to do preliminary test work with greater prairie-chickens from the Great Plains, a subspecies that is not endangered, although it is becoming increasingly rare. The wild population of Attwater's prairie-chickens crashed sooner than expected, however, and there clearly was no time for experimentation. It was time to act.

When we visited the Houston Zoo in early August 1995, keepers Jerry Caraviotis and Oren Dorris showed us the eighteen young birds in a connected series of large cages. Raised on commercial pheasant foods as well as mealworms, crickets, and greens, the wary "teenagers" darted back and forth between the well-sheltered enclosures at our cautious approach.

Caraviotis and Dorris worked out new methods for determining the sex of their young charges at an age of two and a half months. Males are slightly heavier than females, even at an early age, and they begin to lose the barring that marks the outer tail feathers. Careful observation also revealed that they begin to "stomp" while still in juvenile plumage, apparently a prelude to the typical male display behavior. These sexing methods proved highly accurate when correlated with more expensive and time-consuming genetic tests, thereby allowing selection of the individuals destined for release.

Newly hatched prairie-chicken

We viewed, too, the adult flock of seven females and six males in a remote corner of the zoo grounds. As we quietly approached the fenced enclosure, we saw one bird dart for cover, but we could not spot the others we knew to be there. Only when Caraviotis walked into the pen did some emerge from hiding. They get to know and tolerate those who work with them daily but are extremely wary of any strange figure.

This wariness, of course, will help the prairie-chickens survive on their return to the wild. Interns at the zoo have worked to condition them with owl tapes, dogs, and snakeskins, even videotaping their reactions to the threats. Last year, when captive-raised birds in an outdoor pen saw a hawk overhead, they froze and crouched down in the grass, indicating that this is an innate behavior of young birds rather than one learned from the parents.

We returned to the Houston Zoo in mid-August 1995 with personnel from Attwater Prairie Chicken National Wildlife Refuge to watch some of the birds being banded and radio-collared for release. All of them were males, for the decision was made to retain all females in the breeding program for the present.

Weighing from eleven to twelve grams, the collars represented about 1.6 percent of each chicken's body weight, a small burden for so strong a bird. With every transmitter tuned to a different frequency, each individual could be followed in the field. A "four-hour mortality sensor" doubled the signal rate if the bird did not move for four hours, allowing quick location of any dead or dying prairie-chicken.

The males from the Houston Zoo were transported to the refuge near Eagle Lake on August 17 and combined with other chickens from Fossil Rim. They were then released into a thirty- by fifty-foot pen with a chain-link fence to guard against predators and an inner barrier of plastic net to forestall injury to the birds. On August 21, both ends of the pen were opened, and the young prairie-chickens were allowed to wander out on their own into a dense field of soybeans. The recovery program for the Attwater's prairie-chicken had begun in earnest.

Of the thirteen birds released, three were still alive in the wild two months later, according to refuge manager Terry Rossignol. One other bird was discovered to be suffering from dehydration and was returned to the zoo. At least one was killed by a mammalian predator, one succumbed to a fungal infection, and the other birds died of unknown causes, although they showed signs of dehydration in the intensely hot, dry weather.

Although this may not sound like a resounding success, refuge personnel consider it more than satisfactory. "It is a lot better than we expected," says Rossignol. "It is one of the best release results we know of for a grouse species."

The large clutch size of the prairie-chicken clearly indicates that few chicks reach adulthood. Rossignol is encouraged that a quarter of the released birds survived the first few weeks, and he feels that bodes well for the success of the program.

The recovery plan for the Attwater's prairie-chicken calls for the eventual release of six hundred birds a year. That goal is still far in the future, but the cooperative effort offers the last great hope for an otherwise doomed species. The captive breeding program may eventually save the prairie-chicken; however, we must also save the prairie on which it lives.

Clearly, the captive propagation of Attwater's prairie-chickens is possible, but in the few years since the completion of these columns, the wild population has continued to decline. Only the federal refuge near Eagle Lake and a sanctuary near Texas City owned by the Nature Conservancy of Texas still harbor wild birds in small numbers. Through 2002, a total of 554 prairie-chickens reared in seven facilities were released; however, fewer than 50 remain.

There is little suitable habitat remaining on the coastal prairie, and therein lies the secret to preserving the prairie-chicken and other vanishing prairie species. Texas' rarest bird has survived into the twenty-first century, a feat that many considered highly unlikely, but without a great deal of hard work, it may soon join its close relative, the eastern heath hen.

10

A Few of Our Favorite Birds

People often ask us to name our favorite birds, and we find that an all but impossible task. Some merit consideration because of their flamboyant colors; others, because of their unique habits or personalities. Actually, our favorite bird is probably the one we are watching at the moment, for each brings great enjoyment to our lives. The following, however, are a few species about which we have written through the years. Some, such as the northern mockingbird and greater roadrunner, are quintessential Texas birds, ones that we could not possibly ignore without fear of local criticism. Others are those with which we have had personal experiences that etch them forever in our minds. Finally, we have included abundant and widespread birds with which everyone is familiar, the better to illustrate how fascinating those common birds can be.

The Perfect Swimming Machine—Common Loon: 1978/1997

Tucked snugly into sleeping bags in the canoe country of northern Minnesota, we were lost in the deep sleep that comes easily to tired paddlers. Suddenly, the quiet was broken by maniacal shrieks of laughter, and from across the lake came answering cries, as if demented demons were prowling the night. Roused so rudely to consciousness, we felt an instant of terror before we recognized the nocturnal calls of the loons, and we chuckled in delight as we lay listening contentedly to the eerie chorus, slowly sinking back into somnolence.

More than any other bird, perhaps, the common loon has become a symbol of the northern wilderness. Its haunting cries echo across the lakes and through the boreal forests from Alaska to Iceland and southward through Canada to the upper portions of the United States. Scores of wildlife artists have painted its likeness. Its image adorns souvenirs of every description from the resorts and tourist areas of the great North Woods.

One of the most beautiful of birds in breeding plumage, the common loon, *Gavia immer,* is glossy black above and white below. White spots checker the dark back; a collar of white streaks encircles the neck. In the sunlight, the head and neck glisten brightly with greenish iridescence. Swimming on the clear blue surface of a deep glacial lake, surrounded by dark spruce trees and white-trunked birches, the common loon seems the epitome of avian elegance.

Many Texans do not realize, however, that loons spend the winter months in the coastal waters and on large inland lakes throughout our state. Because they are exclusively aquatic, loons must abandon

Common loon

Our Life with Birds

the icebound North in autumn and migrate southward or to the coasts in search of open water. Consequently, the common loon is frequently encountered along our shores and in the bays from late October into April. Many congregate in Galveston Bay and are easily seen from such vantage points as the Texas City Dike.

Unfortunately, the birds we normally find in Texas do not resemble those depicted by most artists. In a postnuptial molt, common loons lose their dapper plumage. Gone is the crisp, clean black-and-white pattern, exchanged for more uniformly dark gray feathers on the head, neck, and back. The birds usually leave again in spring before molting back to courtship attire.

Stilled, too, is the beautiful, melancholy call described by various authors as a cry, a yodel, or an eerie laugh. The loon seldom calls on its wintering grounds, for it uses the wild song in courtship and to proclaim a nesting territory.

Despite its drabber plumage and its silence, Texas' version of the common loon is no less fascinating a bird. A magnificent swimmer and diver, it rides low in the water, diving repeatedly in pursuit of fish that it catches in its sharp-pointed, daggerlike bill and swallows underwater. Indeed, the European name for the common loon, "great northern diver," better reflects its aquatic elegance.

When approached, the loon disappears instantly and can remain submerged for a minute or more, reappearing well out of danger. It seldom flies when threatened, for its heavy body and solid bones, an adaptation for diving, make the takeoff a frantic, scrambling run across the surface. Safety lies in its natural element below the waves.

Loons are, quite literally, swimming machines, streamlined and with their webbed feet located far back on their bodies, the original stern-wheeler paddleboats. Canadian ornithologist and artist Terence Shortt calls their legs "the perfect swimming devices—the most efficient paddles ever developed." The feet are laterally compressed and flare into long, webbed toes. These paddles give a vigorous thrust, while on the return stroke, the toes fold along the knife-edged feet to give a minimum of resistance.

For all their skill in the water, loons are virtually helpless on land. Because they cannot bring their feet forward under their bodies, they waddle awkwardly along, pushing themselves on their bellies. They must build their nests at the water's edge, where they can readily slide on and off.

Migrating birds sometimes land in parking lots and on roadways—perhaps mistaking them for ponds on dark, rainy nights—and once on the ground, cannot take off again. With wingspans measuring as much as five feet, however, common loons are swift and powerful fliers once aloft and have been clocked at more than seventy-five miles an hour during long migration flights along the Atlantic coast.

Five different species of loons compose the family Gaviidae. They range around the Northern Hemisphere, with some breeding in the Arctic almost to the northern limits of the land. In addition to the common loon, others include the Arctic, Pacific, yellow-billed, and red-throated loons. The last three have occurred in Texas but are very rare and difficult to identify in winter plumage. They are listed as "accidental" on the official checklist for the state.

Loons are considered by many ornithologists to be the most primitive of North American birds, tracing their ancestry far back into avian antiquity. Such determinations are highly subjective, but for this reason the loons are generally placed at the beginning of our current field guides, which attempt to arrange the families from the most primitive to the most highly evolved.

In spite of its seemingly archaic lineage, the common loon faces an uncertain future. Pollution and acid rain in once-pure northern lakes have depleted small fish and aquatic invertebrates on which loons feed. Some pairs cannot find enough food to raise their ravenous chicks to maturity and eventually abandon traditional nesting grounds. An increasing number of lakeside homes and cabins, with their attendant boat traffic, also makes it difficult for loons to find the solitude they demand. Oil and chemical spills, too, take their toll as loons spend the winter season along the U.S. coasts.

The common loon clearly warrants our concern, for there is no more elegant or poetic symbol of the North American wilderness. And even in the nondescript winter garb we see in Texas, it proves a fascinating bird, one that is perfectly adapted for the aquatic life it leads.

The Drunken Derelict—Reddish Egret: 1996

A dozen species of herons and egrets inhabit the Texas coast. Few families of birds are as distinctive; few are more elegantly attired. The herons are at their best, however, when the spring breeding season approaches. Extravagant nuptial plumes adorn their heads, necks, and backs. Beaks, faces, and legs glow with neon colors as the hormones begin to flow.

The tall, stately birds stride through the marshes and pace the sandy beaches and mudflats in search of the fish, crustaceans, and other aquatic life on which they feed. Many stand patiently waiting for their prey, heads drawn back, rapier bills poised for the strike.

The reddish egret has little patience with such tactics. Instead, it dashes about in the water on long, spindly legs, shaggy plumes blowing freely in the wind. Leaping comically into the air, it whirls about, stabbing repeatedly after fleeing fish. Wings raised to cut the glare on the water's surface, a trick called "canopy feeding," the egret pauses to watch for movement. Then it is off again at a trot with long, lurching strides, looking for all the world like a drunken derelict.

While most members of the heron family range widely across the country, inhabiting both saline and freshwater habitats, the reddish egret, *Egretta rufescens,* seldom forsakes the saltwater beaches and bays. It is rarely seen inland and occurs in the United States primarily along the Texas and southern Florida coasts. It also ranges south through Mexico and the West Indies. There is no concerted migration, but a portion of the population apparently drifts southward during the winter months, reaching as far as Colombia and Venezuela.

One of the real specialties of the Texas coast, from Bolivar to Boca Chica, the reddish egret attracts the attention of birders from around the world, who come to add this uncommon species to their lists.

Normally, this large, gray heron has a rusty red head and neck, the source of its common and scientific names. Its bill in spring is bright, shining pink with a black tip; its legs are cobalt blue. There

Reddish egret

are no obvious plumage differences between the sexes.

However, a less common white form of the reddish egret is also known. Surveys suggest this white morph accounts for 1 to 4 percent of the Texas population, and it seems to be more abundant in deep South Texas than along the upper coast. Unlike the immature little blue heron, which is white only in its youth, it remains white throughout its life. Although it might easily be mistaken for a great egret, the white-morph reddish egret can be recognized by its shorter stature and flesh-colored bill.

Like the great and snowy egrets, the reddish egret was nearly wiped out by plume hunters at the turn of the century. The elegant birds were killed by the hundreds of thousands and shipped to the East Coast for the millinery trade. It was then fashionable for women to wear large hats decorated with sprays of the filmy nuptial feathers, the "aigrettes," which give the egrets their name. Under this onslaught, the reddish egret disappeared entirely from Florida but has since been reestablished. One Texas colony was apparently overlooked by the market hunters, and the species miraculously survived to become one of the avian jewels of our coastal strand.

Breeding in colonies, often with other herons, reddish egrets prefer to nest in shrubs or clumps of prickly-pear on low islands along the shore. Less frequently, the crude platform of sticks is placed on the ground above the waterline. Some pairs line the twiggy saucer with softer grasses and reeds; others have no time for such refinements.

Males engage in territorial pursuit flights, twisting and turning in stylized battles. The victor then parades back and forth before his prospective mate, beak pointed skyward, plumes fully erect and trembling in a bristling array.

Both partners share in the nest building and in incubating their three or four light bluish green eggs. The young hatch in twenty-five or twenty-six days and are fed a regurgitated soup of tasty marine morsels. Capable of short, tentative flights in about four weeks, they leave the nest area at about forty-five days of age.

Reddish and white morphs pair indiscriminately, and chicks of both colors sometimes occur in the same nest. Occasionally, a dark egret will have patches of white feathers.

On a recent trip with the Spring Branch Science Center to Rockport and the Aransas Refuge, we saw a number of normally plumaged reddish egrets. In full breeding dress, they displayed shaggy manes of cinnamon plumes as they patrolled the shore and cavorted in the shallow waters of the bays.

Our favorite, however, was a white-morph bird standing near a pair of whooping cranes that allowed a close approach. Facing us, no more than thirty yards away, it stared back with an intense, unwavering gaze. A strong wind at the bird's back blew its plumes up into a halo around its face, a punk-rock hairdo that seemed to match the wild look in its glaring yellow eyes. Enthralled, we watched for several minutes, at times nearly forgetting the larger cranes that stood nearby.

Few birds could steal the show from the rare and endangered whooping crane, but a reddish egret always warrants a second look. Both red and white forms are stylishly elegant in their breeding plumage, and they rank among the greatest comic actors in the avian world.

The charming little American kestrel is the smallest of all our local hawks. It also ranks as one of the most beautiful. Although absent from the Texas coast during the breeding season, kestrels return to the Houston area to spend the winter. Often seen perched along power lines and fencerows, they prefer open fields and woodland edges but wander frequently into city parks and vacant lots.

Long, narrow, pointed wings and a long tail mark the American kestrel, *Falco sparverius,* as a member of the falcon family, a worldwide group of more than fifty species long admired for their blazing speed, fierce and haughty beauty, and hunting ability. Ancient Egyptians deified a falcon as the god Horus, and the peoples of central Asia trained falcons to hunt for sport and food as early as 2000 B.C.

This smallest of the North American falcons was formerly called the "sparrow hawk." That name has now been changed to bring it into line with nomenclature used in Europe, where the sparrow hawk is a bird-hunting accipiter related to our sharp-shinned hawk, and the tiny falcons are called "kestrels."

A jay-sized raptor, the American kestrel has a wingspan of less than two feet. The male, the "tiercel" in falconers' parlance, is smaller than his mate, as is the case with most birds of prey. He averages about ten inches in length and weighs little more than three ounces.

Both sexes have russet backs and tails and buff underparts, the only species of small hawk so colored. The female, also called the "hen," is barred with black above; the adult male has a black-tipped, unbarred tail and lighter barring on the back. His distinctive blue gray wings contrast sharply with the otherwise rusty plumage, and his blue gray cap has a rusty crown. Both male and female have two vertical stripes on each side of their white faces, a double "mustache" where other falcons have but one.

The American kestrel ranges widely across two continents, from Alaska to Nova Scotia and southward from the Arctic tree line to Tierra del Fuego at the tip of South America. Scattered populations also occupy portions of Central America and the West Indies. The species normally avoids the Amazon basin and other densely forested regions throughout its range. In the United States, it occurs from high alpine meadows to desert habitats, but prairies, grassy savannas, and farmlands constitute its favored hunting grounds.

Kestrels breed sparingly in the northern and western portions of our state but are strangely absent along the Gulf Coast and in South Texas. During migration and in the winter, however, they withdraw from the most northerly portions of their range and are common throughout the state.

Surveying their territories from wires or the tops of trees, kestrels perch in a characteristic round-shouldered posture, watching with keen eyes for movement below. Launching into flight, they often hover on rapidly beating wings, then plunge feetfirst to pin their luckless prey to the ground with flashing talons.

Grasshoppers, beetles, cicadas, and other large insects make up the bulk of the summer diet, with small lizards and snakes for variety. Small mammals and birds are added more frequently to the winter menu, when insects and other cold-blooded prey become difficult to find.

Kestrels are cavity nesters, utilizing holes excavated by flickers and other large woodpeckers. They may also occupy natural cavities in trees, niches in rocky cliffs, and old buildings. Competition for nest holes is fierce, and the little falcons must vie with screech-owls and other birds and mammals for suitable homes. Harry Oberholser, in *The Bird Life of Texas,* attributes a sharp decline in kestrel populations to loss of tree-trunk holes and to pesticides. During the 1960s and early 1970s, he notes, the species was nearly wiped out as a Texas breeder.

American kestrel

Kestrels readily adopt nest boxes, however, and several regions of the country have embarked on projects to erect suitable homes for these handsome raptors. Some states place houses atop roadside billboards, providing kestrels with ample perches from which to survey their new domains.

The male selects the nesting territory, often returning to the same location year after year. Such site fidelity apparently promotes pairing with the same female, although this is not always the case. The female then begins to associate with her chosen mate, and the two hunt together across the territory, eventually engaging in stylized aerial displays. Ritual courtship feeding by the male further strengthens the bond, and the female follows him as he carefully selects a nest site.

Four eggs compose the average clutch, although the female may lay as few as three or as many as seven. Both sexes incubate, the male sitting more often in the morning and evening. He spends more time on the nest than do males of the larger falcon species.

The young hatch in from twenty-nine to thirty-one days and grow rapidly on the protein-rich diet brought by their parents. They reach adult weight in sixteen or seventeen days and fledge about two weeks later. Efficient parental defense apparently leads to a high survival rate for fledgling kestrels. The pair frequently renests if the first clutch is lost, and second broods have also been noted, particularly in the southern states.

Although the tiny American kestrel may not seem as glamorous as the famed peregrine falcon or its other large relatives, this common little bird of prey is a lovely and welcome addition to Houston's winter scene.

A Feathered Rainbow—Purple Gallinule: 1992

Few people, given the opportunity to design a bird, would have the audacity to invent the purple gallinule.

The head, neck, and underparts of this foot-long, feathered rainbow are bright bluish purple, flashing a variety of iridescent hues in the summer sun. The back is glossy, bronzy green, with shades of blue in the wings. The bright red bill is tipped with yellow and extends up into a forehead shield of pale sky blue. Below this crazy-quilt assemblage of brilliant colors is a pair of long, bright yellow legs and feet, terminating in absurdly long yellow toes.

The gallinule, *Porphyrula martinica,* stalks the overgrown marshes and swamps, using its long toes to walk lightly across the lily pads and floating reeds, constantly bobbing and nodding its head and twitching its short, upturned tail with gleaming white undertail coverts. It normally chooses to swim across patches of open water but, if startled, takes off in labored flight, long legs dangling awkwardly.

It is little wonder that this bizarre and gorgeous bird represents one of the highlights for birders first visiting the southeastern states. Its myriad bright colors hint at tropical origins, and the species ranges from South Carolina around the Gulf of Mexico to Texas and thence southward through Central and South America.

In spite of its seeming awkwardness in flight, it migrates from most of North America in winter, retiring to the warmer climate of the tropics. It also wanders far north of its normal range on occasion, turning up unexpectedly in the northern states and Canada.

The purple gallinule breeds in the eastern half of Texas, westward sparingly to Dallas, Austin, and San Antonio, but is most frequent in coastal marshes. Although it usually winters well south of our state, it may remain in deep South Texas and along the lower coast.

The nest is a crude saucer of grasses, cattails, or rushes, partly concealed by an arching canopy of vegetation and constructed just above the water. A ramp of reeds frequently serves as an approach. The six to ten cinnamon pink eggs are liberally speckled with brown.

Both parents incubate over a period of from twenty-two to twenty-five days, and the downy, precocial hatchlings soon leave the nest to wander through the grass and paddle in the shallows. Some reports indicate the young may be brooded in a second nest nearby.

Purple gallinules sometimes live in small family groups, with the nonbreeding birds helping to defend the territory and feed the hungry young. They are surprisingly noisy, especially in defense of the nest, uttering raucous, laughing cries of *hiddy-hiddy hit-up hit-up.*

Purple gallinule

Their omnivorous diet includes seeds, fruits, leaves, snails, aquatic insects, and frogs, and they have also been found to prey occasionally on the eggs and young of other small marsh birds.

The purple gallinule and its close relatives, the common moorhen and the American coot, often swim like ducks, pumping their heads back and forth as they glide through the water. However, they have chickenlike bills that extend in horny frontal shields up their foreheads, and they occupy a family with the rails.

Coots are equipped with lobed toes for paddling, whereas gallinules have the extremely long, slender toes suited for walking across the floating and emergent vegetation. In summer, they can often be seen wandering about in the marshes of Anahuac National Wildlife Refuge or on Galveston Island, shepherding groups of half-grown young.

The word *gallinule* is derived from the diminutive of the Latin *gallina* and means "little hen." This little hen, with its huge feet and brilliant colors, however, is one of the most striking inhabitants of Texas' coastal ponds and marshes.

A Most Colorful Shorebird—American Oystercatcher: 1997

The American oystercatcher, *Haematopus palliatus,* is one of the most strikingly marked of all our shorebirds and, at eighteen to twenty inches in length, one of our largest. Whereas most of the myriad sandpipers and plovers with which it often associates are modestly attired in shades of brown or gray, the oystercatcher wears more flashy, formal garb of black and white.

The adult has a black head and neck, a dark brown back, and white underparts. Male and female share this characteristic plumage, although the female is often slightly larger than her mate. The bill is a shockingly bright red orange; the legs, pastel pink. Immature birds, however, have dark-tipped reddish bills for the first year of their lives.

In flight, the oystercatcher flashes large white patches in its wings and tail. It can be a noisy bird, uttering loud *pic pic pic* alarm notes and piercing cries of *wheep-wheep-wheep* when it is disturbed.

Pacing the beaches and exposed shell reefs alone or in small groups, the oystercatcher uses its unique bill to pry open mollusks or pick at crabs and marine worms. The bill is long and laterally flattened, with knifelike edges and a chisel tip. Indeed, the formidable weapon has been aptly described as "nature's original oyster knife."

In careful observations of the Eurasian oystercatcher, which some taxonomists consider to be one of several subspecies in a large complex that also includes the American oystercatcher, researchers found that the bird depends on one of two learned feeding techniques. It is either a "stabber" or a "hammerer."

Stabbers cautiously approach open clams, oysters, or other bivalves and plunge their bills between the two halves of the shell before they can close. They quickly snip the strong adductor muscles and then pick out and eat the meat.

Hammerers, on the other hand, employ no such subtleties. They simply pull loose the mollusk and shatter one valve with a series of powerful blows of the chisel-like bill. The bill is then inserted through the broken shell to cut the adductors and pry the two halves apart.

Young oystercatchers apparently learn one of the two techniques by watching their parents, who assist them as they learn to feed.

Unlike many of the other shorebirds, which arrive along our Texas coast in late summer and early autumn after migrating from their breeding grounds in the high Arctic, the American oystercatcher is a year-round Texas resident. It ranges along the entire shoreline but is most common on the central portion of the coast. Confined strictly to a marine environment, it virtually never strays inland from those tidal waters.

A shallow scrape on a sandy beach or shell bank serves as a rudimentary nest, and the olive buff eggs sparsely marked with brown

American oystercatcher

Our Life with Birds

are laid directly on the ground. The normal clutch consists of three eggs; however, if something happens to them and the pair renests, as many birds do, the female normally lays only two more. The eggs hatch in from twenty-four to twenty-nine days, and the downy chicks fly about five weeks after hatching.

Family bonds are strong, and both parents share the incubation chores and the care and feeding of the young. Juveniles take a long time to learn the tricks of opening the bivalves that make up a substantial portion of their diet. This extended period of intensive parental care may be one reason for the small clutch of two or three eggs. Most other shorebirds typically lay four.

American oystercatchers appear to be expanding their range northward along the Atlantic coast. They occur from New Jersey all the way down the eastern coasts of the Americas to Argentina, as well as from Baja California south to Chile on the Pacific side.

On the U.S. Pacific coast, they are replaced by black oystercatchers, *Haematopus bachmani*. This equally striking bird is entirely sooty black, but with the same red orange bill and pink legs. To our knowledge, it has never been seen in Texas.

Although the two North American oystercatchers have very different plumages, they sometimes hybridize where their ranges overlap along the Mexican peninsula of Baja California. Biologists disagree as to whether the two are valid species, merely subspecies, or members of what they call a "superspecies." The last term implies two species of common descent but with different geographic ranges. It is not clear whether they have as yet diverged enough to present biological barriers to interbreeding.

Similar taxonomic problems arise with the classification of oystercatchers around the world. Some authors list a total of six species; others name twice that number. They disagree on whether some of those should be accorded full species status or are merely geographic races of a more wide-ranging species. All are either black and white or entirely slate black, with bright red bills and red eye rings.

Although the exact taxonomic status of the American oystercatcher remains the subject of discussion, modern field guides and the official checklist of the American Ornithologists' Union presently consider it distinct from the black oystercatcher of the Pacific coast.

Whatever its true relationship to others in its family, however, the American oystercatcher should be appreciated as a uniquely colorful and fascinating resident of the Texas Gulf Coast.

Fisherman in Formal Dress—Black Skimmer: 1998

The black skimmers fly just above the quiet waters of Galveston Bay, lower mandibles cutting the surface with their razor edges. Periodically a bird dips its head, beak snapping shut on a small fish. It gulps its catch and rejoins the group, tracing an arrow-straight path across the bay.

The birds fly with carefully choreographed precision, their wing beats seemingly synchronized. Reaching the opposite bank, they wheel on long, narrow wings and sweep low again, retracing their route across the water, intent on more minnows that are attracted to their wakes.

Appetites satisfied, they swirl up from the surface and alight on a sandbar. There they huddle close together, standing on absurdly short legs, bills pointed into the light sea breeze. They seem suddenly awkward and ill at ease on land, but they remain ever dignified in their black-and-white formal dress.

The elegant black skimmer is a common bird along the Texas coast during the summer months but occurs less frequently in winter. It breeds along the Atlantic and Gulf coasts from Massachusetts to the Rio Grande and southward through Central and South America.

Skimmers occasionally wander inland, especially on the winds of summer storms, but most of the North American population remains along the coastal beaches and bays. In South America, however, they range far inland along the major river systems, including the Amazon basin. While northern skimmers migrate southward in the fall, the South American birds time their movements to coincide with the annual flooding of the rivers, dispersing to feed over the shallow, spreading waters.

The black skimmer, *Rynchops niger,* is black above and white below. Its huge, black-tipped red beak is laterally compressed to cut the water like a knife. Juveniles are mottled brown above instead of black, but their profiles remain unmistakable.

The genus name stems from the Greek *rhunkhos,* meaning "beak" or "bill," and *ops,* "the face." *Niger* is Latin for "black." Certainly this "beak-faced" bird is well named scientifically, for its bill is its most distinctive feature. Two other closely related skimmers occupy portions of the Old World tropics, and the three species are the only birds whose lower mandibles are longer than the upper.

Also unusual are the pupils of the skimmers' eyes, which are vertical and quickly narrow to slits in bright light. These function to cut the glare from sunlit water and white sand. In spite of this adaptation, however, the black skimmer feeds primarily by touch, not by sight. It often forages in late evening or at night, perhaps choosing a time when the water is calmer and more fish ascend to the surface from the depths.

Some authorities assign the skimmers to their own avian family, but most combine them in the family Laridae with the gulls and terns. Clearly, their closest allies are the graceful, buoyant terns.

Black skimmer

The black skimmer breeds in colonies on sandy islands, beaches, and shell banks, often in company with local terns and gulls. The nest is a simple, shallow scrape in the sand with none of the grasses that sometimes line the nests of other larids. The three to five large eggs vary widely in color, from white or buff to greenish blue, and are liberally spotted with dark brown. Perfectly camouflaged, they blend with the sand, seashells, and beach debris and can be very difficult to see.

Both parents incubate the eggs that hatch in about three weeks, and the male may play a larger role than his mate. The semiprecocial, downy young are fed on regurgitated fish and crustaceans dropped beside the nest. Eventually, they will accept whole fish, but the lower mandible does not begin to elongate until the chicks are nearly full grown, their shorter beaks enabling them to pick up food directly from the sand.

In defense of their nests, the aggressive adult skimmers stand their ground or swoop low at an intruder, uttering sharp, barking cries of *kak, kak, kak.*

As the chicks begin to wander from the nest site, they hide when danger threatens by scratching hollows in the sand and stretching out flat in them, kicking up sand to partially cover themselves. This may also help to keep them cool in the broiling sun. They can fly about twenty-three to twenty-five days after hatching.

During the nineteenth century, skimmer eggs were collected commercially as food, and the adult birds were shot for their feathers by the plume hunters. Subsequently protected by migratory bird laws, populations recovered nicely. Recently, black skimmers have also colonized southern California around San Diego and the Salton Sea.

Development and increasing beach traffic, however, pose new threats to many of the black skimmer's traditional nesting grounds. Even a slight disturbance in the colony reduces the rate of nesting success. When adults are flushed while incubating their eggs or brooding their young, those eggs or chicks readily fall prey to predators or perish under the hot summer sun.

Occasionally, an industrial plant or coastal community aids in the conservation effort by setting aside and protecting parking lots or other open areas that skimmers have begun to use. Such is the case in the large colony established on the Dow Chemical Company property in Texas' Brazoria County, creating a major tourism attraction and a great deal of goodwill between the company and the environmental community.

Few of our Texas birds are more distinctive than the black skimmer. Although it sports the most unusual profile since Jimmy Durante's, the skimmer graces our bays and beaches with its dapper plumage and aerial elegance.

The Jaunty Paisano—Greater Roadrunner: 1981/1997

Few Texans require an introduction to the well-known roadrunner, one of the most distinctive birds to occur within the borders of our state. The official symbol of New Mexico, it ranges widely across the desert Southwest, from Kansas to California and southward to central Mexico.

Popular in Southwestern art and folklore, this slender, long-legged bird appears on everything from belt buckles to coffee cups, from bumper stickers to comic strips. Legends and folklore abound. It is more formally known as the greater roadrunner, *Geococcyx californianus,* to distinguish it from a similar species, the lesser roadrunner, *G. velox,* that occurs in portions of Mexico and Central America.

The roadrunner is a year-round resident throughout most of Texas but occurs less abundantly in the eastern portion of the state. It dashes across the deserts of the Trans-Pecos, prowls the prairies and red-rock canyons of the Panhandle, and frequents the brushlands along the lower reaches of the Rio Grande. In spite of its western affinities, it may be encountered even among the tall, stately trees of the East Texas Piney Woods.

"It is not much interested in botany," wrote Harry Oberholser. "All it requires is some open space in which to run and scattered trees or shrubs for cover."

Heavily streaked with brown and white, the roadrunner has a long, white-edged tail and a conspicuous crest. The plumage is surprisingly

Greater roadrunner with lizard

iridescent, with greenish tints, but that sheen is seldom seen except at close range. Its bill is long and heavy, and its wings are short and broadly rounded.

In 1903, naturalist Elliott Coues described roadrunners as "singular birds—cuckoos compounded of a chicken and a magpie," the latter a reference to the long tail that serves as a balance and rudder in mad dashes across the landscape.

Although this ground-dwelling bird is fully capable of flight, it takes to the air only under extreme duress. When danger threatens, it prefers to dart off through the underbrush, sprinting at up to fifteen miles an hour. When alarmed or curious, it slowly raises its shaggy crest and tail, uttering an almost dovelike series of cooing notes or loudly clattering its beak.

The roadrunner is a member of the cuckoo family, a large group of more than 120 members that are widely distributed in the Old World. Only a few, however, reside in the United States. These strangely disparate species included the sleek, streamlined, brown-and-white cuckoos; the black, parrot-billed anis; and the roadrunner. Although these may seem at first to be very different in appearance, there are many anatomical similarities. All are relatively slender birds with long, floppy tails and large beaks. They also have two toes pointing forward and two back, leaving X-shaped tracks in the dust, whereas the perching birds typically have three toes forward and one back.

Many members of the cuckoo family are brood parasites, laying their eggs in the nests of other birds. This trait, however, is less prominent in New World species.

Roadrunners apparently form lifelong pair bonds and remain together even after the breeding season, defending their territories throughout the year. In courtship, the male parades before his mate with head held high and wings drooping. He then spreads his tail and sings his cooing song, perhaps cementing the bond by presenting her with a lizard or other tasty morsel.

The roadrunner eats almost anything that moves—insects, spiders, scorpions, lizards, rodents, and small birds. It is also famous as a snake killer. Legend has the roadrunner building a fence of cactus pieces around a snake so that it cannot escape and eventually impales itself on the spines. Although that technique is obviously fictional, the bird's quick agility lets it capture rattlesnakes and other highly venomous prey. Darting in to stab a snake's head, it then grabs the squirming reptile in its powerful beak and thrashes the snake on the ground.

According to several field studies, about 90 percent of the greater roadrunner's diet is animal matter, and fruit and seeds make up the other 10 percent. The latter consists in large part of ripe cactus fruits that are abundant throughout much of the bird's preferred habitat.

Mated roadrunners conceal their nest in a low tree, shrubby thicket, or clump of cactus. Built of sticks, the structure is usually lined with leaves, grasses, roots, feathers, mesquite pods, and even a snakeskin or two. Both parents incubate the three to six chalky white eggs, although the male normally sits much longer than his mate, especially at night. Experiments show that an incubating male maintains his normal body temperature while on the nest, whereas the female and other nonbreeding males allow their temperatures to drop through the night in order to conserve energy.

The helpless, altricial chicks hatch in about twenty days and are absurdly homely little birds. They grow rapidly under the care of their attentive parents, however, and are capable of flight at about eighteen days of age. Soon after that, they begin catching their own food.

Regional names for the roadrunner include "paisano" and "chaparral cock." Texas author Roy Bedichek, in his wonderful *Adventures with a Texas Naturalist*, wrote that he preferred the name "paisano" because it was so euphonious and because "often in the lonely desert, where company is scarce, this large and lovely bird will travel along with you for miles, staying only a few yards ahead." The name, Bedichek noted, suggests congenial companionship and fraternization, "a fellow countryman or fellow traveler."

The roadrunner often runs beside a vehicle traveling slowly down a country lane or scampers ahead of a hiker along a desert trail. Even though it seldom takes flight, it seems somehow supremely confident in its speed afoot. Tiring of its game, it then darts off into a mesquite thicket or cactus patch, perhaps stopping briefly to look back, raising its long tail and rakish crest in a jaunty avian salute.

A Comical and Curious Bird—Groove-billed Ani: 1987/1997

The groove-billed ani must surely rank as one of Texas' strangest birds. A member of the cuckoo family, this all-black, jay-sized bird has a long, graduated tail and at first glance might be mistaken for one of the ubiquitous great-tailed grackles that roam our state. However, its absurd, almost puffinlike beak is laterally flattened and deeply ridged, imparting a comical air to what Texas ornithologist Harry Oberholser called a "lizardlike facial expression."

Adding to the comic effect are the ani's loose-jointed actions. It flies weakly with a rapid flapping of its short wings followed by a long glide. On landing, its long, floppy tail often flies up over its head, almost knocking the ani from its precarious perch. It looks, quite literally, as if it is falling apart.

The groove-billed ani, *Crotophaga sulcirostris,* ranges from the Rio Grande Valley southward through tropical America to Peru. Although it normally breeds in the United States only in deep South Texas, it wanders sparingly up the Gulf Coast to the Houston-Galveston area and even into Louisiana. There are also sporadic records for other portions of the state, and in spite of their awkward flight, anis have turned up as far away as Minnesota.

Although most species migrate toward warmer climates for the winter, the groove-billed ani tends to disperse northward after the breeding season. These wanderers then spend the fall and winter months in thickets and tamarisk mottes all along the Texas coastal plain.

The name "ani," pronounced "AH-nee," comes from the Brazilian Tupi Indian word for the bird. The genus name, *Crotophaga,* means "tick eater"; the specific epithet, *sulcirostris,* comes from the Latin *sulci,* meaning "furrows," and *rostris,* or "bill." Thus, the groove-billed ani takes both its common and scientific names from the shallow grooves on the surface of its beak. However, these are visible only at close range and may be lacking entirely on young birds and a few adults.

Groove-billed ani

A second U.S. species, the very similar smooth-billed ani (*C. ani*) of southern Florida, has an even higher beak, but without the characteristic grooves. Because the normal ranges of the two do not overlap, there is little chance for confusion. There are a few unsubstantiated sight records of the smooth-billed ani for the upper coast, but the only ani to be expected in Texas is the groove-billed.

Some references state that anis commonly perch on the backs of cattle to pick off ticks, hence the genus name. Other authors assert that such behavior is rare. This, and other habits of the curious anis, seems to vary with the region in which they live.

Oberholser notes that in Texas the ani prefers the "thickest thornbrush it can find," while in Mexico and Central America it is more at home in grassy pastures with scattered bushes. Many birds in the latter regions do feed around cattle, catching insects chased up by the grazing animals.

A steady diet of grasshoppers, termites, roaches, spiders, and even small lizards serves to sustain the ani, but seeds and fruits may also be included. It is this omnivorous feeding behavior that enables anis to move into colder climates in the winter, when insects are normally difficult to find.

Groove-billed anis are extremely gregarious and often gather in small flocks. Sitting motionless in thickets, they betray their presence with a repertoire of soft, liquid, gurgling notes and a chorus of two-syllable calls usually described as *tee-ho* or *pee-oh*. When disturbed, they utter harsh alarm cries and flutter off in their frantic flap-and-sail manner.

Even during the breeding season, when most other birds defend individual territories, anis may band together in small groups of two to four pairs. Some pairs nest alone, but others build bulky communal nests of dead twigs lined with green leaves. All members of such a group participate in building the structure, and all females lay their three or four pale bluish eggs in that single nest. Both males and females then take their turns at incubation, but the dominant male does all of the nighttime incubation and brooding of the young.

In spite of this apparent cooperation, female anis sometimes employ means to increase the probability that their eggs will be the most successful ones in the communal clutch. One strategy is to toss the eggs of other females from the nest. In spite of the competition and occasional conflict, however, research has shown that multipair groups fledge more young per adult than do single pairs nesting in similar habitats.

Incubation requires only thirteen or fourteen days, and the newly hatched, altricial babies are blind, naked, and helpless, with parchmentlike black skin. Growth is surprisingly rapid, and the young are soon scrambling about in the foliage, clinging awkwardly to the thorny branches with both feet and beaks. Within six days they are able to leave the nest, although they may return to sleep for a few more days. Some are capable of short flights at about ten days of age and can fly well in another week.

Even though neither the awkward hatchlings nor their jet-black parents will win awards for facial beauty, the unusual appearance and comical habits of the groove-billed ani make it one of Texas' most distinctive species.

The Epitome of Grace and Elegance—Scissor-tailed Flycatcher: 1978/1996

Flocks of colorful birds stream along the Texas coast in spring, making their annual migration flight from tropical America to their nesting grounds across the United States and Canada. Few of these Neotropical migrants, however, can match the subtle beauty and graceful elegance of the scissor-tailed flycatcher.

After spending the winter months in Mexico and Central America, scissor-tails move northward across the plains, ranging from southern Texas to northern Kansas. Inhabiting open fields and pastures, woodland clearings, and farms and ranches, they fan out across our state to nest and raise their young. They are common summer residents throughout most of Texas east of the Pecos, but appear less frequently in the far western corner of the state.

Officially designated the state bird of Oklahoma, the scissor-tailed flycatcher, *Tyrannus forficatus*, is equally popular south of the Red River. Here it was sometimes called "the Texas bird of paradise" by early settlers.

Certainly we have not forgotten our first encounter with a scissor-tail several decades ago. Newly arrived in Texas in 1960, we went out on a warm May afternoon to wander through the countryside. Along a quiet country road in Chambers County, we found our first scissor-tailed flycatcher perched on a barbed-wire fence. As we stopped to watch, he darted up to catch a fluttering grasshopper in his beak. In flight, his incredibly long, black-and-white tail scissored open and closed, and we thought we had never seen so splendid a bird.

We followed close behind him for half a mile as he moved along the fence, flying out several times across the field and returning to his perch. His upperparts were pale pearl gray, his whitish sides flushed with salmon pink.

Then, in response to a female scissor-tail sitting nearby, he began a spectacular courtship display. Rising high in the air on fluttering wings to reveal their orange red linings, he stalled at the top of his rise and then performed two complete backward loops and a sweeping dive. Pulling out just above the ground, he flared his streaming tail and settled gracefully back on the wire.

We had no way of knowing if the potential mate was suitably impressed, but we were instantly in love. Our fascination has not diminished to this day.

The scissor-tail's beauty belies its pugnacious personality. It fiercely defends its territory against all intruders and does not hesitate to pursue a pass-

Scissor-tailed flycatcher

Our Life with Birds

ing crow or hawk. Swooping repeatedly amid a tirade of shrill, bickering notes or harsh cries, it pecks at the subject of its wrath until the harried and less mobile target is only too happy to beat a hasty retreat.

Such behavior is characteristic of the family known as the "tyrant flycatchers." More than 360 species inhabit the Americas from Alaska to Tierra del Fuego, with most of them in tropical regions. They tend to perch in an upright posture on exposed tree limbs or wires and fly out to catch passing insects in the air. Their heads are proportionately large and often slightly crested, and they have broad, flat bills surrounded by long rictal bristles, or "whiskers," that help to funnel insects into their gaping mouths. Small prey is captured with an audible snap of the mandibles; larger insects are carried back to the perch and beaten on a limb until tender enough to swallow.

The family includes not only the birds we call "flycatchers" but the kingbirds, wood-pewees, and phoebes as well. With a few notable exceptions, most wear drab plumages in shades of brown, greenish, or gray. Some, in fact, are so similar in appearance that they must be separated primarily by voice and present some of the most difficult of all identification problems for the birder.

Not so the scissor-tailed flycatcher, for it is in a class by itself. Noting its elegance and beneficial habits, Harry Oberholser wrote of it: "Its colors are beautifully blended and its movements graceful; from the viewpoint of the farmers and ranchers, it is one of the 'good guys' because it downs a lot of big, harmful insects. . . ."

In addition to catching flying insects in midair, the scissor-tail frequently descends to the ground to capture grasshoppers, beetles, and caterpillars. There it carefully elevates its long tail, keeping the delicate feathers out of the dirt. A few berries supplement the diet, but flycatchers are largely insectivores.

The female scissor-tailed flycatcher is somewhat duller in color than her mate and has a slightly shorter tail. Otherwise, the sexes look much alike.

After courtship, the female constructs her grass-lined cup of twigs and weed stems on a horizontal limb or in the crotch of a tree or shrub. There she incubates her three to six eggs alone. Creamy white or pale pinkish, the eggs are lightly and beautifully mottled with various shades of red, brown, gray, or olive.

Hatching in from fourteen to seventeen days, the ravenous young consume vast quantities of insects brought to the nest by both attentive parents. The young birds fledge at about two weeks of age, but it will be some time before they acquire the long, streaming tail feathers of adulthood.

Scissor-tailed flycatchers may nest from late March into August in Texas and inhabit elevations ranging from sea level to more than four thousand feet in the western mountains. Then, as the days shorten into fall, flocks of the graceful birds begin to assemble, lining the roadside fences with autumn elegance. Slowly they work their way southward across the Rio Grande to spend the winter amid tropical riches. When spring comes again, however, the scissor-tails reappear, bringing with them their unique brand of avian beauty.

Everyone's "Robin Redbreast"—American Robin: 1995

The dawn chorus begins haltingly at 4:30 in the morning, just as the eastern sky begins to turn a pale gray. Soon the music swells to fever pitch as the horizon brightens and more and more birds join in. It would be difficult to sleep late during midsummer in Minnesota's great North Woods, but there are few places more enchanting to spend the longest days of the year.

Black-capped chickadees sing their names repeatedly from the spruce outside our cabin, and chipping sparrows perch on the sill to pick insects off the windowpane. Above the twittering songs of the goldfinches and the nasal, tinhorn notes of a white-breasted nuthatch, the melancholy calls of the loons echo across the lake.

Then, just outside our door, we hear a particularly loud, liquid song we do not recognize. Peering out, we discover a male American robin serenading us from the limb of a white-barked birch. The music is rich and melodic, described by one field guide author as *cheerily cheer-up cheerio.*

We are embarrassed that we did not recognize immediately this icon of North American bird life. Arguably, the robin is one of the best known of all our birds. Except for our periodic northward excursions, however, we seldom hear its lovely song.

As we watch, the robin throws back his head and sings again, a challenge to all within range of his powerful voice. His brick red breast is a diagnostic field mark, of course, but equally striking are his coal black head accented by white eye ring and throat and his gleaming yellow bill.

Too often we forget how beautiful the common and widespread American robin, *Turdus migratorius,* really is. We see it most often as it hops around our Texas yard in the wintertime, part of a foraging flock in search of insects, worms, or berries to sustain it through a hostile season. Often in drabber plumage, and silent except for repeated *tut tut* calls, the birds then act like small passerine chickens. On its breeding grounds, however, the robin undergoes a metamorphosis. Here, in its true element, it is one of our premier songbirds, deserving of widespread acclaim.

Returning home later in the summer, we pay a visit to the Houston Zoo. To our great surprise, we find robins to be much more common there than ever before, apparently nesting in the trees and shrubs around the beautifully landscaped grounds. This is a relatively new development in local ornithology. Through the years, we have seen occasional nests in the Houston-Galveston region, but most of our winter robin population departs northward in the spring.

Harry Oberholser notes that in historic times the robin was only a local breeder in Texas, primarily in the forested northeastern portion of the state. Most of Texas was too hot, dry, and bare to provide suitable habitat. Between 1925 and 1940, however, there was an increase in tree planting and lawn sprinkling in local communities, resulting in well-spaced trees, higher humidity, and the requisite mud for nest construction. Breeding robins then increased in North Texas and spread sparingly south to Waco, Austin, and San Antonio, reaching Corpus Christi along the coast by 1967. This season's abundance of resident robins at the Houston Zoo in Hermann Park can probably be traced to similar changes, with more attention paid to

American robin

adding landscape plants and increased watering.

The robin's nest is a solid fortress of grass and mud, which the female shapes with her breast and wings by turning round and round in it. A lining of softer fibers cushions the three to five eggs of clear "robin's-egg blue."

One of the robin's endearing traits is its penchant for nesting near human habitation. Seemingly undisturbed by urban activity, it may select a backyard fruit tree or a sheltered window ledge as readily as a pine on the forest's edge. Around the country, we have seen nests in city stoplights over busy intersections, on the newly hung rafters of a barn under construction, and under the raised cowling of a farmer's tractor.

Hatching after twelve to fourteen days of incubation by the female, the young robins leave the nest at fourteen to sixteen days of age. They bear little resemblance to their parents, and their liberally speckled breasts betray their familial relationship to the thrushes.

Adult American robins are gray brown above, with brick red breasts, white bellies, and black-striped white throats. Older males, like our Minnesota songster, often have black heads, contrasting strongly with the white eye ring and yellow bill, but there is a great deal of individual color variation, and the sexes cannot be safely separated by plumage alone.

To most of us, this familiar bird is simply "the robin," but it is more properly called the American robin. Other robin species, in the genus *Turdus*, inhabit Latin America and the Caribbean islands, and one, the clay-colored robin, is seen regularly in Texas' Lower Rio Grande Valley.

Our Life with Birds

The American robin was named by homesick colonists for the robin that occurs commonly throughout Europe. The two species are only distantly related and do not really look alike, but both have red breasts.

Our robin ranges across the entire length and breadth of the continent and serves as the state bird of three different states—Connecticut, Michigan, and Wisconsin. It nests from the tree line in Alaska and northern Canada south to the Gulf Coast and into the mountains of Mexico.

Withdrawing from the northern portion of its range in winter, the robin migrates southward to seek more abundant food supplies. Its return to the North is widely heralded as the first sign of spring, although less popular birds may actually precede it on the migration flyways.

The American robin is many things to many people. In our area, it is primarily a winter resident, more common in some years than in others, perhaps because of variations in the natural food supply. However, a few individuals now remain to nest, a welcome development that adds a lovely songbird to Houston's summer scene.

The Many-Tongued Mimic—Northern Mockingbird: *1979/1992*

On January 31, 1927, the Texas legislature unanimously declared the mockingbird our official state bird, adopting a resolution presented the previous November by the fifty-thousand-member Texas Federation of Women's Clubs. The mockingbird, the legislature noted, "is found in all parts of the State, in winter and in summer, in the city and in the country, on the prairie and in the woods and hills, and is a singer of distinctive type, a fighter for the protection of his home, falling, if need be, in its defense, like any true Texan. . . ."

Who, among Texans, could not select the species on a list of favorite birds after such accolades? However, people of other states apparently shared this enthusiasm, for Florida, Arkansas, Tennessee, and Mississippi made it their state bird as well.

The mockingbird does, indeed, live year-round across all of Texas and ranges widely over the continent, from southern Canada to Mexico and the West Indies. Several other mockingbird species occur in Latin America, however, necessitating the full name of northern mockingbird for our resident species. The scientific name is *Mimus polyglottos*, the "many-tongued mimic." It shares the avian family Mimidae with more than thirty species worldwide and ten that occur regularly in North America, including the gray catbird and eight different thrashers. All tend to be long-tailed, with short wings and slender, slightly down-curved bills.

Mockingbirds form long-term pair bonds and show unusual fidelity to their mates. They may, however, establish individual feeding territories during the winter months. The diet is almost equally divided between insects and fruit, and it is the presence of the latter in the form of wild berries that allows the mockingbird to remain throughout the winter when many other insectivores move southward. Then, in warmer seasons, it devours great quantities of beetles, caterpillars, and grasshoppers. Although the mockingbird is occasionally an unwelcome poacher of cultivated fruit, its eating habits are in general beneficial.

The male begins to build the twiggy, cuplike nest, and the female lines it with softer grasses and plant fibers, laying three to five bluish green eggs spotted with brown. She incubates for about twelve days, and both parents feed the young that leave the nest some twelve days after hatching. The male may then take over care of the fledglings, while his mate begins a second brood. The pair will raise at least two broods a year, sometimes three or four in the southern portions of their range. Fiercely aggressive and territorial, mockingbirds do not hesitate to attack in defense of their eggs and young, dive-bombing intruders of any size.

Dull gray above, with white outer tail feathers and white patches in the wings, the northern mockingbird is not particularly colorful, but it makes up for that with its amazing vocal talents. Early naturalist John Burroughs called it "the lark and the nightingale in one." Mark Catesby, who encountered the mockingbird in South Carolina and wrote the first scientific description of it, noted that the local Indians called it *Cencontlatolly,* or "four hundred tongues."

It imitates other birds so expertly that sound spectrographs show the renditions to be almost exact duplicates, and it also mimics other creatures and mechanical sounds. Squeaking hinges, chimes, and barking dogs are well within its vocal range. A famous mockingbird at the Boston Arboretum was heard to reproduce "thirty-nine bird songs, fifty bird calls, and the sounds of a frog and a cricket."

One New York City bird reproduced perfectly the "beep-beep-beep" of a backhoe in reverse; another threw a high-school football game into confusion by mimicking the referee's whistle. Yet another joined the National Symphony Orchestra during an outdoor concert in Washington, D.C., imitating the flute that imitated the bird calls in *Peter and the Wolf.*

The mockingbird repeats each phrase two or three times before moving on to the next. In the spring and early summer, it may sing

Northern mockingbird

for hours, both day and night, particularly if the moon is bright. Both sexes also sing in the fall when they are claiming feeding territories.

The exact purpose of the mockingbird's mimicry is the subject of argument among biologists. Mimicry normally connotes deception by the mimic, either as a defense or in competition with others. However, most of the mockingbird's vocalizations are unlikely to deceive anyone, particularly in combination with all the other unrelated phrases.

Some suggest that a larger repertoire may improve the bird's ability to attract and stimulate a mate and to intimidate rivals. One way of increasing the size and diversity of that repertoire is to learn and incorporate sounds from the surrounding environment. In short, the mockingbird simply adopts new sounds that it hears in order to add variety to its song.

Whatever the motive, the "many-tongued mimic" delights Texans across the state with its aggressive antics and its cheerful, rollicking song.

ISBN 1-58544-380-8